It's Time To Get Selfish

A journey inside of Self...a fascinating truth...
a life altering experience...

Robyn Busfield

Ingrid,
Wishing you a wonderful journey

RBfield

Published by:

Buzzworld Publishing
P.O. Box 75
Hermosa Beach, CA 90254

For information
please visit:

www.itstimetogetselfish.com

If you are unable to purchase this book from your local bookseller, you may order by visiting:
www.itstimetogetselfish.com
(International orders may also be placed via this site)

Library of Congress Catalog Card Number: 2006908474
ISBN-13: 978-0-9787984-5-1
ISBN-10: 0-9787984-5-7

First paperback edition: December 2006
Printed on acid-free paper
in the United States of America

<u>Dedication</u>

This book I dedicate to my parents,
Peter and Carmel Busfield.

In memory of my father...

With his wisdom, love, warmth, and support, my father
led me through childhood with an amazing ease.
As I became a young woman, he watched with pride.
As I spread my wings, he allowed me to fly.
Dad, I feel your Spirit today and I know you are with me.

To my mother...

With her tremendous amount of passion, strength, and faith,
my mother has always set an amazing example of
will to succeed. She is always there for me, offering love
and support the way only a mother can. I couldn't ask for
a better mother...and friend.

Acknowledgment

I would like to thank my parents, Peter and Carmel Busfield, for gifting me with the freedom and will to search for the tallest mountains, the courage to climb them, and the love to take the rise and fall.

In acknowledgment of my sister, Susan. She is one-of-a-kind…no matter how tough things may get, she always knows how to smile and make me and the world smile with her. Also, I would like to make a special mention of Susan's husband, Wayne, and send warm wishes to my nephew, Aaron.

I would like to thank my brother, Peter, who is always willing to extend a helping hand and provide loving support wherever he can. A special thanks to Peter and his wife, Natalie, for their heart-felt efforts and involvement in the final stages of *It's Time To Get Selfish*. Also, I would like to send warm wishes to my niece, Jessica, and a big welcome to her new brother, Jayden.

I would like to make a special mention of my Nanna, who at 92, sets an amazing example of love and strength for all her children, grandchildren, and great grandchildren.

With many special thanks to Janet, Nancy, Jennifer, Suzan, Irene, and Steve. Your tremendous amount of support, encouragement, input, and friendship while preparing the finalized message of *It's Time To Get Selfish* will never be forgotten.

In appreciation of all my dear friends here in America, thank you for your ongoing love and support while writing this book. I would like to make special mention to Anna and Helen for delivering those life altering messages throughout my searching years. Thank you for being there and for making a difference in my life.

I would like to make a special mention of my friends in Australia, who have grown with me even in my absence. Thank you for being there for me when my father passed; and to those who traveled a long distance to provide loving support. I am blessed to share such true friendships.

And finally to you, the reader, though we may not have met, I thank you for joining me on this journey.

With much love and gratitude,

Robyn

CONTENTS

INTRODUCTION

Come share with me a journey inside of Self, where you will discover a fascinating truth, a magical experience, and a life you forgot you had the ability to create...

Through extensive research, I have been blessed to uncover the knowledge that leads to our Natural State of Peace, Spiritual Freedom, and Ultimate Happiness that we all do crave. This knowledge is extensive, however, if you are prepared to search beyond old habits of belief and accept this journey into a new light of awareness, then a life altering experience full of fresh imagination, within a realm of unlimited possibilities, will be yours to harvest.

Each and every one of us at birth is naturally gifted with life's golden keys. These keys are designed to assist in unlocking our creative talent and supply us with all life's glories and riches. They are designed to connect us to our Natural State of Wellness and Ultimate Happiness. All that you ever desire in a lifetime is naturally at your fingertips. Each one of us is born with free will to utilize these golden keys, *or not*. Through society conditioning and conforming belief patterns, many of us have chosen through an unaware state to set aside these golden keys. Meaning, over great lengths of time, these keys have simply become discarded, and then forgotten. These keys, however, are not lost. They remain at your fingertips 24/7. The choice is yours now to take hold of these keys and unlock the door to uncover a life that you simply forgot you had the ability to create. To remember it the way it was supposed to be.

My wish is to offer you a rebirth of inner power and enlightenment, equipped with a pure understanding of these golden keys, so that this time you *will* unlock the door to your Natural State of Wellness, Ultimate Happiness, and Creative Talent. So that this time you *will* encounter life as you were originally designed to come forth and encounter it.

First, you must take the time to nurture Self with the love and time that Self deserves. Unfortunately, starving love from Self has been our largest downfall throughout the ages, and has assisted in bringing us to the position of lack in most areas of our life. Taking this time out means getting *selfish* enough to put Self first for a while. Filling up your own cup first, so you truly have something to go out and give to this world. Now is the time to take hold of those golden keys, polish them, and reach higher than ever before, unlocking the gateway that leads to your greatest potential.

But first…*It's Time To Get Selfish!*

It's Time To Get Selfish

It's true they say the pearl is within,
It manifests within us and ignites every grin.
I'll develop the pearl that's deep within me,
And emanate my beauty to all that I see.
Happiness, laughter, and magical grace...
Will be my existence and light up my space.
In fulfilling my own needs and all that I wish,
I'll utter the true love of my own bliss.
It's time to get selfish and it's time to give me...
The love that ignites me and all that I see.

In respect of every Soul and its intimate connection to All-That-Is, I have chosen to capitalize the word "Soul" throughout this book.

Names have been changed within stories and dialogues to protect parties involved.

I hope you enjoy *It's Time To Get Selfish.*

Part 1

INTRODUCTION
TO SELF

***

Providing love for Self is an honest
act of selfishness…

Chapter 1

Self-Awareness

WHAT IS SELFISHNESS?

Selfishness today, for the most part, is viewed as a negative expression by society. We are taught that too much focus on Self is not in alignment with our greater power of giving. If we have no idea who we truly are within, what our passions and desires are at a Soul level, and what connects us to that eternal happiness, then how can we even begin to understand the power of giving? If we are unable to understand or give to ourselves, how can we honestly and freely give to any other?

In today's society, many are depriving themselves from taking the time out to provide for their own happiness. Sadly, many of us don't take a good look at who we are at a Soul level and what we truly want in this life. We are too caught up in the approval of others to ever really seek approval from where it matters most—*ourselves*. We have been led to believe that happiness is derived from *out there*. Happiness that is true, concrete, and eternal is always from *within*. No other can know our inner desires that form our true happiness.

It's Time To Get Selfish

It is true that we long to see peace, happiness, and love all around us. We want to see our loved ones happy. We can assist in providing happiness to others, but when another's happiness becomes more important than our own, we are depleting ourselves and in essence end up not having anything to give. On the other hand, when we look to make ourselves happy *first,* we are filling up our own cup of love, which then naturally overflows to all those around us.

Few of us get selfish enough to learn to accept, enjoy, and truly love who we are.

When you deplete Self and feel unhappy in Self, you attract more of the same. You've heard, "like attracts like" right? Makes sense that you will attract unhappy people, who then in turn will want you to make them happy, and so you do, and then here you go again. Does this sound like your life? Do you find yourself often pleasing another before pleasing yourself? As you begin to find your own love and happiness inside, you will automatically find happy people all around you. For as "like attracts like," your "happiness will attract happiness."

Would you like to find true happiness within and all around you? Can you imagine always feeling complete, free, and totally happy within? When you are feeling this good, do you know what this is called? The answer is self-love!

It's now time to take a fresh look at selfishness and redefine it from a positive standpoint. Selfishness is taking the time to explore your own desires. Trusting in your own decisions. Trusting in your own happiness.

4

Knowing that for you, the answer is *within* every single time. Becoming *selfish* enough to make *you* happy first!

Selfishness is giving to Self.

Throughout this book, we are going to focus on the positive aspects of selfishness and learn how to implement this as a loving art into our lives. To endeavor in finding our inner peace, inner freedom, inner happiness, and inner love that is our Natural State of Being. It is my aim to unfold my research of this knowledge to you—knowledge that will provide you with the ability to regain a connected state with your true Self, thus providing an alignment for receiving all that you desire every day of your life.

Are you ready now to embark on this life altering journey inside of Self—to explore life and discover the inner power that is naturally yours—to live like you came here to live? If you are, you must be prepared to open new doors and walk into new horizons. You must be prepared to forget what you were told and allow yourself to remember what you already knew. Ready? Okay, *Let's Get Selfish!*

TRUSTING IN SELF

Can you imagine trusting one hundred percent in all of your own decisions? Trusting that the ultimate answer is *within* each and every time? The problem for many of us is that we have been taught to look *out there,* as we, ourselves, are not enough to provide such knowledge. The truth is that each and every one of us has our very own answers *within,* and is fully equipped with Universal information of our every right.

Mankind is made up of basically two uniforms, the outer being the physical and the inner being the Soul. The physical we know is truly our body, but what about the Soul? Have you ever wondered what your Soul is? And what its true value is to you in this life?

As we all know, when we think, our thinking is coming from the brain, being the physical. But have you ever stopped to consider where your *feelings* are coming from? Do you recall a particular event where you had excited feelings prior to the event? It may have been a school dance, or it may have been the launch of a new business venture. Did you follow your inner feelings toward this event?

On the other hand, do you recall having a warning gut feeling about a particular situation? Not those fearful stage feelings, but where you could feel something was ultimately wrong. It may have been a business opportunity you were offered, or it may have been a weekend trip you were invited to with friends. Did you follow your inner feelings in regards to this event?

As you recall these inner gut feelings you have received on various occasions, have you ever stopped to wonder *why* you received them…or *where* they came from?

Feelings are delivered via a Spirit-linked energy, or in other words, that inner part of us that we name our Soul. This energy has also been offered a variety of other names; for example, Inner Being, Inner Wisdom, Inner Voice, etc. It doesn't matter what you name it. As long as you understand we are talking about this energy that exists as an inner part of you, which is unavailable to the naked eye, and is truly a part of YOU every single day of your life. Throughout this book, we will refer to this other part of us mostly as our "Soul" or "Inner Guidance."

Our Soul offers guidance in every step, but unfortunately, for many of us, we have been looking *out there* and not trusting what our Soul, our best friend, is trying to reveal.

PAYING ATTENTION TO GUT FEELINGS

Gut feelings are guidance from our Soul.

There are two types of gut feelings:

- A warning gut feeling

Our warning gut feelings let us know when we are in *miscreating* mode. Each time we receive a warning gut feeling, it is revealing to us that what we are focusing on, or the direction we are heading, in that instant, is not in alignment with our greater desires. It is advising us to *let go* of what we are currently focusing on and shift our focus elsewhere, or, take note of the direction we are heading, and then seek to change our direction.

- An uplifting gut feeling

An uplifting gut feeling is providing us with information to advise us that we are moving forward in a positive fashion. It is letting us know that what we are focusing on, or the direction we are heading, in that moment, is beneficial toward our pre-desired path.

Every time you make a decision, your Soul provides you with a gut feeling to let you know whether you have made the right choice for your highest good. You may call it a gut feeling, gut instinct, hunch, or just a feeling you get. It is all the same. All types of inner feelings are offered as guidance from our Soul.

When we understand that gut feelings are information we are receiving from our Soul, we can then appreciate their true importance. For many of us, we receive these gut feelings and are so used to ignoring them that we aren't always aware they are there. The truth is, these gut feelings are vital to our everyday survival of life. When we adhere to these feelings, we are being led toward happiness, peace, love, passion, etc. When we ignore these feelings, we move blindly toward whatever is in our way.

Each time you get a gut feeling of any kind, you are receiving intuition. Your Soul might be trying to tell you, "Hey, it's down this path, go this way." Then a buddy comes along and says, "Where are you going? It's over here!" So you follow his advice, only to end up complaining later that you should have done what FELT right in the beginning! Do you recall situations where this has happened to you? Take a few moments to recall situations where, if you had paid attention to your Soul, things would have unfolded differently.

As you pay more attention to your gut feelings, you will naturally become more aware each time a new one surfaces. Each gut feeling will appear stronger than before. Then, in time, you will find it difficult to ignore them.

Our Soul provides us with guidance through feelings 24 hours a day. It feeds us with information even in our sleep, thus being our dream state. We will cover "receiving through our dream state" at length later in this book.

Your Inner Guidance is the most important part of your decision making 24 hours a day!

It was many years ago that I began to recognize the importance of gut feelings in my own life. I started to question where gut feelings came from, and why they appeared to deliver information that was crucial to our everyday happiness and survival. I decided to obtain any information I could in relation to the topic of gut feelings. At that time, I was residing in Sydney, Australia. I searched many a bookstore for any type of information on gut feelings. I was led to a variety of books, each offering some form of guidance relating to our Inner Awareness. However, I could not locate a book or any tools that would lead me to a *deeper* understanding of our gut feelings.

A few months later, I awoke one day to a gut feeling that felt something like a gentle nudge to move to America. As the days passed, the gut feeling continued to surface. I began looking into what the move to America would entail. At the time, I was happily set in Sydney, with a great job, wonderful family and friends, and was living in a comfortable home. But deep down on some level, I felt I had to go to America. At the time, I did not know the reason behind the gut feeling. I just knew in my heart that I had to go.

I picked myself up and landed in sunny California. I didn't know why I was there, but nonetheless, it became a great experience and quite the adventure. A number of months passed by, when one day, a good friend placed in my hand a tape relating to our *Inner Guidance*, produced by Jerry and Esther Hicks at "*Abraham-Hicks Publications." This tape included a complete description on how and why we receive gut feelings! At last, and when I least expected it, here was the information that I had been praying for. I was soon led to many other fascinating tapes in the Abraham-Hicks library. This was the day my life would change forever!

Am I ever so glad I listened to that continual, inner, gentle push that sent me packing to sunny California. To my knowledge, at the time, when I received these first tapes by "Abraham-Hicks Publications," they were not readily available in Australia. Had I ignored my inner gut feeling and not moved to America, it may not have been possible for me, at that point in my life, to receive this extremely important life altering information.

Learn to accept and enjoy this Inner Guidance that you have. It is this other Spiritual part of you that lives on for all eternity. It knows ALL that you have ever desired and all that you will ever desire. It knows the past, present, and future make-up of who you truly are! Know that *within*, you have every single answer you could ever need to walk this path with peace, love, and prosperity. You have one hundred percent guidance right at your fingertips! Trust this Inner Guidance that loves and adores you and is always with you. It may take a little time to understand and completely trust, so allow yourself patience to regain this wonderful consciousness in your own time.

*Abraham-Hicks Publications P.O. Box 690070 San Antonio TX 78269
www.abraham-hicks.com

Self-Awareness

GETTING TO KNOW SELF

Mankind is made up of basically two uniforms, the outer (physical) and the inner (Soul). These two uniforms come together to *evolve* through the process of *creating*. Let's take a look at each one's role in the creative process:

Physical: The work of our physical counterpart, our human form, is to utilize the power of thought to deliberately create the existence as one wishes to be, do, and have. Focused thought is a form of *asking*, as in the biblical term "ask and you shall receive." To create abundantly and productively, the physical counterpart must pay attention to the feelings provided by the Soul, and then be led by these feelings toward actions that will lead to manifestations. Learning to let go and have faith is required along the way. The last step is to reap and enjoy the manifestations. With fresh manifestations in existence, from a new time and place, the physical counterpart continues to create beyond that stand. (Our creative potential is discussed in detail in Part Two of this book).

Soul: The work of our Soul is to provide feelings to guide the physical to its creations of desire. The Soul will lead to all that is positive. It naturally disconnects from all that is negative. The physical will only be led by the Soul to positive creations. When a thought or choice is processed by the physical, the Soul always follows with a feeling. If the thought is a good thought and is in alignment with your desires, you will receive an uplifting feeling. If the thought is a negative thought and is not in alignment with your desires, a negative feeling will be felt.

When we are thinking (physical), we are in "asking mode."

When we are feeling (Soul), we are in "receiving mode."

We are indeed Creators. We only need to *ask* and we shall *receive*. Our Soul, our best friend, is with us all the way to assist us in creating the life we came here to create.

Our Soul is a make-up of energy—pure, positive, loving energy. This pure, positive, loving energy is what we feel within our bodies when we are *connected* to our Soul.

Negative energy is the feeling that arises when we feel disconnection from our Soul. It is not the Soul that initiates the disconnection. Our Soul is always available within us and wants to feel the connection to its human form. It is our human choice of awareness, via focused thought, that either connects us to our Soul or disconnects us.

Each focused thought initiates connection or disconnection.

Our Soul connects to us through a vortex of energy. A vortex of energy could also be described as a lifeline of energy. When our focus is positive, the positive energy we are emanating naturally keeps our vortex open, and the like positive energy of our Soul flows smoothly through. When our focus becomes negative, it slows down the positive energy flow moving through the vortex. As the negative energy is increased, the positive flow is decreased, causing a stronger disconnection. It is similar to the operation of a fire hose. If we kink or bend the fire hose, the water flow is interrupted. When the kink or bend is strong enough, it can stop the flow of water altogether.

When we choose a positive thought, we *feel* a positive feeling from our Soul. This is our connection point. The stronger the positive thought, the stronger and nicer the feeling becomes, thus the stronger the connection.

On the other hand, when we choose a negative thought, we begin to *feel* a negative feeling. This is our disconnection point. The stronger the negative thought, the stronger and more uncomfortable the feeling becomes, thus the more we are disconnecting.

These two feeling points of connection or disconnection are less noticeable to us when we are not paying attention to them. Paying more attention *out there,* rather than paying attention *within,* has softened this awareness. For many of us, we are moving through our day unaware of what we are creating or miscreating in the moment.

We all have the ability to easily sense another individual's connection state or disconnection state. Many of us appear to be better at reading another's energy rather than reading our own. This could be due to the fact that we have been taught to look *out there* at another's happiness much of the time, thus providing us with a stronger awareness of another's connection point rather than our own. For example:

- "Her Soul is shining through."
  (We are sensing the strong connection in another)

- "That one doesn't have a Soul."
  (We are sensing the disconnection in another)

Much of the time we are focused *out there*. We are focused on other people's business. We are focused on other people's problems. We need to get in touch with our own business. We need to get in touch with our own problems.

It is in our quiet time that we begin to understand Self. It is through quiet time that we learn to engage in our true connection. I'm not saying we must always be *within* and never be *out there*. We must balance our focus. It is important to find balance in both areas. We must find ourselves some quiet time to turn within and get to *know* Self. To interact with other people is also important to our growth. However, until we connect with Self and find our truth within, we really have very little to offer others.

LET'S GET CONNECTED

To get better connected and to understand the guidance we receive from our Soul, we must take quiet time and go within. Quiet time can be found by taking a walk along the beach or a walk through the park. When we are alone, feeling relaxed, and at peace, we are then able to better connect and receive uplifting energy and guidance from our Soul.

To work at strengthening your connection state, I suggest using a daily meditation technique. Meditation can be beneficial, as it encourages us to engage in an *ongoing* connection with our Soul. When we connect with our Soul, we feel truly alive. As we take the time to get to know our Soul, our Soul will shine through as much as we invite it to.

Self-Awareness

Here is a meditation technique you can use daily if you wish:

Meditation Technique: Fifteen minutes per day is a good amount of time to set aside for this exercise. Choose a position to sit, either on the floor or in a comfortable chair. Keeping your back upright throughout the process will assist you in breathing deeply and easily. Turn off background noise, such as the television, phones, etc. Throughout the meditation exercise, it is important to clear your thoughts. Paying attention to your breathing will assist in clearing thoughts.

Begin with some deep breathing. Each time you inhale and exhale, pay attention to your breathing. As you exhale, know that any previous tension is now leaving your body. Feel yourself begin to relax toward a calm, peaceful state. Allow your breathing to relax and regulate. Feel the presence of your body by noticing any tingling or slight body movement. Take inventory by feeling your skin, your hair, your fingers, and your toes. Continue to pay attention to your breathing. Take some time to enjoy this relaxed, calm state—the connection you are now sharing with your Soul.

This meditation process will assist you in recognizing the true connection point with your Soul. It will also assist you in understanding and receiving Inner Guidance and wisdom in a more profound way. If you grant yourself this meditation time every day for a minimum of two months, you will gain the ability to receive guidance from your Soul more readily and effectively on a daily basis. After two months, daily meditation might not be so much of a requirement. At that point, once or twice per week may be sufficient to remind us how important and fulfilling it can be to find that *ongoing connected state.*

Becoming more familiar with your connected state through meditation will assist you in understanding how your connection point *feels* while going about your daily life and interacting with others. You will also naturally become more *aware* each time a disconnection occurs within, and you will quickly be able to identify the current thought that is causing the disconnection.

How connected you feel on a regular basis will determine how often you require meditation time to assist in maintaining that healthy connection place. Once you reach a healthy connection place a majority of the time, you may find it appropriate and more enjoyable to just take some walks alone on the beach or in the park a couple of times per week, in lieu of meditation time. The important point here is: gift some quiet time to yourself to assist in maintaining a healthy connection. Or in other words, get *selfish* enough to take the time to better connect!

Decide what is best for you. However, I do recommend using this meditation technique for the first couple of months to find and understand the feeling place of *true connection.*

FOR BETTER OR FOR WORSE

How magnificent to connect with this wonderful friend that exists inside of us. And to know this friend is with us until the day we die, helping us every step of the way, for better or for worse!

If we are feeling down and in a negative place, it's okay. Our Soul is still there to connect with us whenever we are ready. Our Soul will connect as soon as the vortex is relieved to allow the connection to take place. It is our physical choice, each and every moment, to invite the connection or to disallow the connection. We have free will in every stance. It is our choice entirely.

Our Soul is always ready to connect when we are. In other words, when we give up control—for example, when we learn to let go of frustration, worry, or anger— we naturally begin to relax and connect. It is then that we get closer to this wonderful friend and our vortex to this lifeline of Spirit becomes strengthened.

When we let go and listen to our Soul's advice and stop trying to take control of situations, we open a stronger, wider vortex, making the information clearer and more precise than ever before. When we have *faith* in the information that we are receiving, a whole new world of possibilities opens.

Start by practicing daily on the smaller events to enable your trust to surface. When confronted with decisions during the day such as, "where you will go for lunch," or "where you will go that evening after work," try to listen to that inner gut feeling. Get used to that inner gut feeling and its purpose. You will begin to find that each decision you make, based on the way that you *feel,* will lead you to the best possible outcome.

Pay attention each day as you go about your decision-making. If you have ignored a gut feeling, see how that event turns out. Take notice as often as you can. It will soon become natural for you to follow your gut instinct on almost every occasion.

When you are connected to your Soul, not only do you feel wonderful within, but you are also gifted with one hundred percent guidance each and every day! Staying *connected* is the first golden key. Trust and allow your Soul to guide you. Get to know this inner friend, the friend that is truly YOU. The friend that wants you to shine and be as joyous as you came here to be!

Chapter 2

Breaking Down the Walls

FINDING THE WAY

As a child, I was blessed to have the freedom of adventure that unfortunately many children today do not. I was able to climb the tallest trees, run through pastures filled with horses and cows, and venture for miles along running creeks while collecting tadpoles and mulberries. I was able to share joyous adventures with other children who shared the same freedom. For the most part, children today are kept away from that freedom. They are blanketed and protected through fears that have been imbedded into society.

When children are born, they come into this world vulnerable, innocent, and extremely loving. As children grow in society, many are warned to "be careful of this" and "watch out for that." Many are taught to be aware of their surroundings. Over the years, they are then faced with losing their innocence and sincere loving ways due to the imbedded fears that are offered by society.

As children are continually warned to be careful, they begin to put up walls to protect themselves and include the energy of *fear* into their surroundings. They begin to fear certain events, situations, and people. Over the years, walls become concrete. A blockage to some desires and experiences becomes a given. It is then that they begin to question, "How do I become a happier person? How can I create more *love* in my life?"

We are unable to *invite* free, loving energy on a regular basis when we are unable to *give* free, loving energy on a regular basis. We attract what we give. It is a given.

There are two energy types that we have the ability to offer. These two energies are *love* and *fear.* When we emit *love,* we attract back to us that same type of energy. When we emit *fear,* we attract back to us that same type of energy.

We attract circumstances to us through the energy we are emitting, LOVE or FEAR.

The answer is to break down those walls we have built around us, so we may attract the ongoing true love that we are longing for in our lives. To break down those walls, we need to release built up negative energy. In other words, we need to *heal* the inner child. We need to retrain our thoughts so we begin to believe there is much good *out there.* We need to understand how to take responsibility for what we are attracting into our lives. We also need to take a few deep breaths and relax into the knowing that all is truly well.

SHIFTING AND HEALING ENERGY

To get closer to our true selves, it is vital to heal wounds that have built up over the years via painful experiences.

Breaking Down the Walls

We each have the power within to assist ourselves in healing wounds from the past. This process of healing and shifting old unwanted energy won't happen overnight, but with a clear intention and mindset, the energy will certainly shift at a greater pace. Clear intentions always assist in painting a smoother, easier, and quicker path toward one's goals. Once you begin this process of healing old wounds, negative energy will begin to shift and leave your presence. You will begin to feel more alive and free as you go about your day, with less confrontations, less anger, less sadness, less fear, and less pain. You will find conversations you hold with others to be considerably more uplifting.

When we are holding on to past negative energy that we haven't dealt with, it stays with us and reappears in our everyday life situations.

Let's take a look at an example:

Sally found she was being confronted with people on a regular basis who appeared to be very nosy, wanting to know about her business way more than she cared to discuss it. She would get annoyed and frustrated on the inside, while trying to remain calm on the outside. She would always find that she would leave the conversation with a sick feeling in her stomach. She didn't know why. Sally saw her friends discussing their business with each other and very happy in doing so. She witnessed it over and over. Sally knew she had an issue with this particular topic and that it was eating away at her more than she cared to feel.

Sally took pen and paper and some quiet time. She decided to get to the bottom of this and free herself once and for all from this negative feeling that was surfacing almost on a daily basis. She began by writing how it bothered her when people expressed an interest in her personal life. She wrote how frustrated she became and how she wanted to walk away every time this happened. Next, Sally began to write how she wished to *feel* when people would confront her with personal questions. She wanted to *feel* good when others showed an interest in her personal life. She wanted to share gleefully of herself. She wanted to *feel* open to express herself honestly and freely. She wished this more than anything. Finally, she *asked* to feel free and open when communicating with others from that day forward.

Sally wrote about this topic each day for about twenty minutes before retiring. She continued writing for one week. In the weeks that followed, Sally noticed her attitude was changing. She could feel a shift in her own energy. She was feeling more positive and confident about herself and her personal information. Sally wrote in her journal from time to time as the change took place. She would write how she was noticing the difference and how happy it made her feel. Also, how she wished to continue to release the old negative feelings until she was totally free.

In the months that followed, Sally was feeling a complete turnaround. She was holding lengthy conversations with others about her personal life that felt positive and uplifting. She was beginning to enjoy sharing of herself and sharing in deep conversations about almost anything. Sally was delighted with her results. People were truly enjoying Sally's presence and Sally was also enjoying theirs.

What turned personal conversations into a delight for Sally was that first of all, Sally made the decision to change her attitude. Second, Sally took the time to write and work at releasing the old energy. As Sally wrote about the problem, she was identifying the problem. As she wrote about the new attitude she was wishing for, she was in that moment letting go of the old energy and replacing it with a new, desired energy. Writing about it as well as staying focused helped Sally to shift the energy more rapidly.

If you have situations repeating in your life that have an ill effect on your energy, write each situation down. When you have your quiet time, sit down and spend some quality time to deal with each subject. Work on each subject separately. Decide in the beginning that you will get to the bottom of the problem and release those ill feelings. Always start by describing the issue at hand. Describe how it makes you *feel*. Explain why you feel bothered by this particular event. If it involved a certain person or persons, write down why you feel annoyed with them. Allow the feelings to arise and jot them all down. When you have established the way you *feel* about this particular subject, the next step is to decide how you wish to *feel* about this subject the next time a similar one arises. Do you wish to *feel* good? Do you wish to handle the situation differently next time? If so, *ask* to feel good and *ask* to respond differently. It is important to be very clear on how you wish to *respond* and *feel* when a similar situation arises in the future.

If you write as Sally did each day, as time goes by, you should begin to feel a sense of relief. As more time passes, the ill feelings should begin to diminish. Continue writing on a regular basis until you feel much better. If you notice a change but still feel some negative energy within, continue to write when you can, *asking* to feel better about the subject at hand. Always try to take notice of the way that you *feel*.

Let's take a look at an example of how Toby shifted his energy:

When someone pointed out to Toby how he should handle something, or what decisions he should be making, he felt annoyed and controlled. Toby recalled, as a teenager, when many decisions were made for him; such as what subjects to take at school, what friends to choose, and how short to cut his hair. He remembers feeling annoyed when he wasn't allowed to make his own decisions. Today, Toby continues to feel annoyed when he feels others are trying to make decisions for him, when of course, he could just thank them and ignore their opinion if he chooses. Toby didn't like *feeling* annoyed and upset with other people. He had seen his friends react differently when they received similar suggestions, taking them with a grain of salt.

Toby decided to use an alternate technique other than shifting his energy through his writings. Toby decided to use his visualization technique. He replayed both of his parents sitting with him on the sofa at home when he was fourteen years old. He visualized them telling him how smart he was and what great decisions he made. They also asked him what subjects he would like to choose at school, how short he would like to cut his hair, and which friend he would like to take on their next camping trip. This helped Toby to remove the old energy of feeling controlled, and to replace it with a new energy of feeling

24

trusted. After a number of sittings, feelings began to resonate within Toby that his parents did trust him to make good decisions. This in turn enabled Toby to feel that same trust in himself. As Toby began to believe in himself and his decision-making, he felt a new sense of pride and inner strength.

Toby repeated the same visualization technique in other areas where he was continually feeling hurt and unworthy. Soon Toby began to feel the old energy of unworthiness shift and the burden lifting from him. He noticed a considerable difference in his everyday life.

Today, Toby feels a strong level of trust in himself. When another offers an opinion, he listens and appreciates their input, knowing that the final decision will ultimately be his own.

It is important to understand that energy does not have to be shifted and moved from its time of origination. It is never a requirement to go back and find the original point where the energy formed. Toby used the visualization technique in relation to his parents as that memory had stood out in his mind for many years, and he could recall this situation very well. All energy can be transformed from its current stand. If a situation happened in recent weeks or even days that didn't feel so good and it was connected to a reoccurring issue, you can use that recent scenario to visualize and/or write to transform the energy.

As you visualize or write about any ill feelings that exist, keep in mind that simply *asking* for the opposite of the ill feelings, or in other words, *desiring* a fresh, positive result is the key to achieving a positive outcome. Naming the issue helps to realize the problem and bring the feelings to the surface, but the *desire* for the *change* in attitude and feelings is always the key.

Our overall energy make-up is formed from the way that we *feel* about ourselves. The way that we *feel* about ourselves determines our entire surroundings. Our overall energy make-up determines which situations or circumstances we will *attract* in every step. Our energy make-up is changing continually based on our fresh attitudes we take on board. The way that you reacted to a situation yesterday determines the type of situation you will attract tomorrow.

Others see us the way we see ourselves. We are constantly revealing to others how we *feel* about ourselves. When you visualize or write about how you would like any past outcome to now represent itself, you are shifting an old awareness and replacing it with a new awareness. This new awareness now attracts a different awareness from others; because this new awareness is causing your energy to now vibrate differently, which causes others to attract to you and view you in a whole new light!

Let's take a look at an example of how Samantha shifted her energy:

Samantha wanted to heal from a past relationship that had left her in a great deal of pain. She still blamed her ex-fiancé, Tim, for certain ways he had treated her toward the end of their relationship. When Tim finally broke off their engagement, Samantha was very distraught. She felt abandoned and alone. Her heart was broken for quite some time. She had felt fearful ever since of having another relationship and taking that risk of ending up with a sore heart again. Samantha decided she wanted to heal and learn to love again.

When ill feelings exist toward a partner from a previous relationship, it is difficult to move forward and release that partner with love. The best way to deal with this painful type of energy is to see beyond their physical and go straight to the Soul level. When we look through to the Soul of a person, we only see beauty. At a Soul level, each Soul is pure, loving energy.

Samantha decided to use her visualization technique. She set aside some time and found a quiet room in her home where she could relax. Samantha visualized meeting with Tim on a beach near where she lived—a place she loved and that also felt comfortable to her. Samantha looked at Tim beyond any of the physical aspects, as she knew him. She felt through to his Soul. In that moment, she could feel his true love for her. She told Tim of the pain she still felt from their relationship. She explained some circumstances where she was still left blaming him. Then she explained some situations where she was feeling guilty for certain ways she had treated him. Samantha told Tim she understood that their time together had come to an end. She also told him how she wanted to now forgive him and also forgive herself. She understood that both of them gave what they knew how to give within the relationship, and carrying on with bitterness was only hurting herself and nobody else. Samantha told Tim that she was truly happy to have shared a special part of her life with him. She also told Tim that she cared for him and wished him a future filled with happiness. Samantha visualized Tim responding with love and understanding. They both hugged and said good-bye.

This was not so easy for Samantha to visualize the first time, though she could feel herself begin to view Tim in a slightly different light than she had done in the recent past.

The next day, Samantha went through the same process and visualized meeting with Tim at the beach. She saw through to his Soul, felt the love once again and then the feeling of completion, as she knew they both had come together for that period of time. And for reasons beyond her knowledge, their time now was to continue in their new directions of desire.

After a few weeks of visualization sittings, Samantha began to finally feel free of this painful energy that had burdened her for too many years. She realized it was indeed possible to move on with her life and remember this past relationship with sincere loving feelings.

If you have a desire to heal old wounds from a past relationship that you have been carrying around, do this exercise as often as you feel necessary. It can assist in healing deeper wounds no matter how they are related. If time permits, a combination of the visualization technique (Samantha's) and the writing technique (Sally's) on the same relationship topic will assist in shifting and freeing up unwanted energy more rapidly.

Don't let negative energy control you. When you notice the same ill feelings coming up again and again, realize that you have the power to release them. You have the power to say *no* to what you don't want, which in turn makes room for what you *do* want! As you work at releasing and therefore no longer owning those heavy, ill feelings, you make room for positive energy to arrive.

Remember, we have developed these ill feelings over many years of our life and now we can release them. As the ill feelings arise, name them and write how you wish to no longer own them. Then write how you wish to *feel* when similar situations arise in the future.

When dealing with any past or current painful experiences, remind yourself that it is truly not your concern how an outsider views you. How another individual *feels* about you can only affect them, not yourself, unless of course you *allow* it to. On the other hand, how you *feel* in regards to another individual can only affect you, not the other, unless of course they *allow* it to.

You deserve to feel good each day. Painful baggage does not need to continue to exist. It is all a matter of choice, and a matter of being *selfish* enough to place the time aside because your true happiness and sense of freedom is worth it!

ENERGY TRANSFORMATION—A FRESH
MAKEOVER

Each one of us owns an energy make-up. This energy make-up is formed from attitudes and feelings we have developed from all of our life experiences.

Each time we come into contact with another individual, parts of our energy make-up are revealed. Another may feel the energy we offer as positive, or it might be felt as negative, depending on what we are *feeling,* therefore emanating in that moment. We all have intuitive abilities and are able to read energy in each other. Whether the

person sitting opposite us is speaking or is silent, the
energy they are emanating in that moment is revealed.

Take a pen and some paper. We are going to complete an
exercise that will reveal to you your weaknesses and
strengths within your own energy make-up. It will also
help you to discover just how many of the qualities you
desire to see in your partner that exist or do not exist
within yourself. If you are currently in a relationship, list
the qualities you appreciate or would like to see more of
in your partner today. If you are currently single, list the
qualities you would desire to find in a potential partner if
you were seeking one today. If it is your desire, you may
also choose a family member, a co-worker, or any
individual you come into contact with on a regular basis.
Some qualities you list, for example, could be honesty,
integrity, sociable, independent, or faithful. Take your
time and list as many as are important to you.

Next, you are going to take the first quality on your list.
We will pretend it is "honesty." Ask yourself the
question, "Do I have this quality? Am I an honest
person?" Answer each question as honestly as you can. If
you believe you are honest some of the time and not so
honest other times, mark that one with a star. That one we
will revisit. Move to the next item on your list and do the
same thing. Ask yourself the question and once again try
to be as honest as you can. If you believe you have that
quality, place a check next to that item. Complete all the
items on your list until you have placed either a check or
a star next to each item. It can be interesting to find that
certain qualities we seek in a partner might actually be
nonexistent within ourself.

Breaking Down the Walls

Okay, now for the next step. We are going to take a closer look at and complete some energy work on each item you have placed a star next to. Let's take a look at the first item with a star on your list. We will pretend again it is "honesty." On a new sheet of paper, you are going to write, "I want to be an honest person." Let's say the next item with a star is, "a good listener." You will then write, "I want to be a good listener." Complete the same statement for each item with a star on your list.

Each time you write a statement of desire from these items, read the statement out loud and with passion. It is important to truly *feel* the desire, so you may attract and become this quality that you are seeking in your partner. For when you emanate the quality you are seeking in a mate, by the magnetizing power within the Universe, you must align to and attract a similar energy type into your world. As you *feel* about Self, so you will attract!

Repeat this same process two times per day, for the next seven days. Complete your "I want" statements from the same items on your list. On the eighth day, you are going to again write each statement, but you are going to change each statement to become "I am" statements. For example, "I want to be an honest person" will now read, "I am an honest person," and so on with each item on your list. Each time you write your statement, read each one out loud. Once again, it is very important to truly *feel* the words as you express them. *Feel* that you *are* the quality as you express it. Complete the "I am" list two times per day, for the next seven days. If you don't find the time to complete your list two times per day, you can spread it out over a few weeks; though try to complete the "I want" list at least twelve times over, and the "I am" list at least twelve times over.

The reason we start with "I want" and then shift to "I am" is because saying "I want" is a closer energy alignment to the energy of "not having," which is the energy alignment of today. It is not so easy to make an energy shift in one big step from not having to having. To shift energy is far easier to accomplish when the energy is shifted in steps. Saying "I want" is not a drastic energy shift, it is an easy, one-step energy shift toward the larger energy step of actually "having." Once the energy has shifted one step with the "I want" statement, we are one step closer to the energy alignment of the desire. We then move to the "I am" statement, which is the larger step and an aligning step with the actual desire. It takes time and some dedication to shift energy, but if you follow these simple steps and apply the right amount of positive focus and passion, the energy will soon shift toward your goal.

This exercise is one you can utilize again and again throughout the years. If you are currently in a relationship, this exercise will help you to evaluate if you are actually emanating those same values that you are expecting and desiring from your mate. If you are not emanating certain values, then you cannot expect your mate to be aligning with you and delivering something to the relationship that you are not. Individuals change over the years as new attitudes and outlooks develop because of surrounding circumstances. As you and your mate are changing, you may feel a shift or separation in energy occur between you. Completing this exercise and applying fresh positive attitudes can assist to buffer your alignment in energies, thus strengthening any weak areas that may have arisen during the relationship.

If you are in a relationship that you are questioning, this exercise can also determine whether or not this relationship is one that is fulfilling your needs. As you begin to emanate the qualities you have been working on, you may or may not receive these same qualities in your mate. Remember, nobody is perfect—you will not line up precisely with a partner because there will of course be variances. You will need to decide if the qualities you seek, that your partner does not possess, are mandatory qualities and if you can or cannot live without them.

If you are not in a relationship today and are seeking a mate, this exercise can assist in attracting the mate you desire. Aligning your energy with the qualities you seek will bring your energy to a whole new level, naturally attracting to you the mate that also emanates these wonderful attributes.

This exercise is an excellent tool to assist in bringing harmony to all of our relationships, whether it is a partner, family member, co-worker, or a friend. However, as we can clearly see here, bringing harmony into our lives always begins with *Self.*

A wonderful book I recommend, which provides tools to assist in reprogramming addictive behavior is *The Power of Unconditional Love* by Ken Keyes, Jr. Visit: www.members.aol.com/inossence

Chapter 3

Finding Self-Love

SETTING BOUNDARIES

A boundary is a guideline for others to see and understand the values and respect we hold for Self. A boundary is a choice for Self that we implement and then maintain. When we implement a boundary, we are expressing *trust* in our own choices. We are expressing a mark of our own self-worth. We know we have healthy boundaries in place when we make loving, firm decisions to stay true to ourself and our own happiness.

Let's take a look at how Christy had difficulty maintaining her boundary:

Christy had decided to go on a camping weekend with four other friends. She was very excited to get away for the weekend. They filled their backpacks and took to the mountains. The first day was magical. The sun was shining and the air was fresh and peaceful. Christy, Mark, and Joel immediately found some pre-planned walking trails and hiked most of the afternoon, while Todd and Carol opted to stay by the campsite and fish in the nearby river.

34

The following day, Todd was up early and was antsy to go hiking. Christy was also up early, so Todd asked her to join him. Christy told Todd she didn't feel like hiking early that morning. Todd didn't want to go hiking on his own, so he pleaded with Christy. Christy said she really didn't feel like it, but maybe later in the day she would. Todd persisted in asking Christy to join him and wouldn't let up. Christy finally said, "Okay, if it will make you feel better that I join you, then I will."

They gathered their backpacks and picked a trail not far from the camp. It was a pretty morning, the birds were singing and the air was crisp. They had been hiking for a while when they came upon a fallen tree. This tree was very large and had landed directly across their path. Todd helped Christy climb up over the tree. When Christy was edging down the other side, she slipped and fell, and somehow landed sideways twisting her right ankle. Christy was instantly in a lot of pain. She tried to stand on her foot, though it was way too painful to place even a slight amount of pressure on. Christy and Todd were at least a mile from the entrance of the walking trail. Todd called Mark from his cell phone. It took Mark a good half an hour before he reached them. Christy's pain was increasing by the minute. Together, Mark and Todd helped Christy back to the campsite. Due to her intense pain, they had to rest every few minutes. It took more than two hours to return to the campsite. When they arrived, Christy was exhausted and in a lot of pain.

Christy recalled earlier that morning when she really hadn't *felt* like going for a hike. She remembered that gut feeling. Now she knew why she *felt* a strong feeling to stay behind. How she wished she had listened to her gut feeling and not been talked into going for that hike!

I am sure most of us can relate to Christy's story one way or another. Christy allowed her boundary to be overstepped, as she had stated her feelings and then overlooked them to please another before herself, therefore not adhering to her own personal choice.

It is important to trust in our own choices and to own them no matter what another may say. If someone else disagrees with our choices, or puts us down for our choices, we must be strong enough to stay *true* to our own choices each and every time. When we have firm boundaries in place, we are saying, "This is me, this is who I am. I trust in all my decisions. I feel happy with my choices."

It can be difficult at times to stand by our word when another is pleading to go "their direction." Of course we would love to make them happy. We have been taught forever and a day to make another happy before ourselves. However, as we saw in Christy's final choice to hike that second morning, it is not beneficial to go against our own inner gut feelings. These gut feelings are there for a reason. They are there to guide us away from events like Christy's misfortune. It is *our* choice in every moment to listen and be led. Christy cannot possibly blame Todd for pleading and wanting her to join him in his hiking. Todd was initially coming from a place of love in wanting Christy to join him. Todd didn't know and couldn't know what Christy's gut feeling was trying to tell her.

A gut feeling always stems from *within* to lead the person who is receiving the signal. We each have our own guidance system to answer our very own questions. Though Todd was initially coming from a place of love, can you imagine how he felt later? Most likely not so good, as he had talked Christy into joining him and later witnessed her in a great deal of pain.

If Christy had followed her own feelings, she would have stayed behind and saved herself from a sprained ankle. Todd may not have been too happy in that moment of Christy sticking to her initial decision, but he would have gotten over it and also learned to respect Christy's decisions. And I am sure he felt a lot worse with Christy's sprained ankle than he would have if Christy didn't go on the walk with him.

Many have been taught to plead as Todd did. For many of us, as young children, it was revealed when we pleaded long enough that we would sooner or later get our own way. It worked! So why not plead as adults? It is coming from an inner child act of knowing we can get our own way when we keep trying. It is not exactly the healthiest place to come from, but nonetheless, we have been taught that it is okay and that it works. See, Mommy and Daddy didn't have very good boundaries either. And most likely their parents didn't have very good boundaries. Though, no one is to blame of course—and the tie can be severed! It is *our* choice to apply boundaries and teach our children or our grandchildren that boundaries are indeed a mark of self-respect.

How many times have you given in to make someone else happy and then later wish you had done what you originally preferred to do?

Let's now take a look at an example of Brandon maintaining his boundary:

Brandon set his dates for a business trip to London. He was going to London to meet with new clients. Kimberly, a very good friend of Brandon's, who also worked for the same company, asked him to alter his schedule to fit in a sales call on her behalf. Kimberly explained to Brandon that she was unable to make a trip to London that month, and it would mean a lot to her if Brandon would call on this one customer. It could also mean a nice bonus check. Brandon explained to Kimberly that he had a very busy schedule on this trip and wasn't able to fit in any more sales calls. Kimberly pleaded with Brandon, offering him half of the bonus check. Brandon knew he would be helping his friend considerably; though, if he went ahead and altered his schedule to fit in her sales call, he had a chance of losing a large account he had recently acquired. Brandon apologized to Kimberly and explained that he would love to help her out; however, he really wasn't able to fit her sales call into his pre-arranged schedule.

We can feel the strength in Brandon's decision here. Maintaining boundaries is most important in maintaining our self-worth, which assists in forming our self-happiness.

The most loving thing we can do for ourself and any other is to follow our own Inner Guidance. When we follow our Inner Guidance, we end up going the right way every single time. It is there for a reason...and a very good reason. Boundaries support us in listening and adhering to our own guidance system. Without boundaries, we can be walked all over, we get talked down to, and there is little or no respect. Every individual deserves respect. Respect starts from within. If we do not respect ourselves, how can we expect another to show us respect?

Work on your boundaries today. Decide who you are and what makes you happy. Then be strong and implement all that you have chosen. When another pleads for you to look their way and make them happy first, work at staying true to yourself. Remember, fulfilling your own happiness first allows your love to grow within, then overflow and emanate to the world, providing others with *your* happiness. It is not your responsibility to make another happy. However, it is *your* responsibility to provide for *your* own happiness.

When boundaries are in place, our happiness falls into place!

COMPROMISING WITHIN BOUNDARIES

Boundaries are an important aspect of our self-worth. It is important we maintain our boundaries and stay true to ourselves. At times though, especially within a committed relationship, we can be tested when two people are having a conflicted feeling toward a certain decision being made. When this happens, we *are* able to compromise with one another without either party losing their boundaries.

Here is an example of Lisa and Scott compromising within their boundaries:

Lisa and Scott had been married for five years. They lived in a small city on the outskirts of Sydney. Lisa had always had a dream of living at the beach. Lisa felt a desire one day to move and thought how wonderful it would be to move to one of her favorite beach areas. Lisa told Scott how she felt. After considering her request, Scott told Lisa he was happy to move, however, he really didn't *feel* like moving to the area that Lisa had suggested. Lisa asked Scott where he felt like living. Scott's reply was to move back to the area they had initially come from—where Lisa and Scott had both been raised. Most of their family and friends still lived in that area. Lisa took some time, checked in with her *feelings,* and soon realized that her feelings to move were partly because she loved the beach, but the thought of selling their home and relocating was also a strong desire. Lisa really did love the area where they had both grown up, so Scott's offer did *feel* good to her. Lisa agreed with Scott that this was a good idea. The next weekend, they revisited their hometown and began searching for their new home.

This story is a great example of compromising within boundaries. As you can see, Scott thought about the move and how it made him *feel*. For some reason, he did not feel good about moving to the beach area. Scott maintained his boundary here and followed the way that he felt. He knew this move sounded important to Lisa, so he offered an alternative that hopefully Lisa would like and one that would *feel* good to them both. Lisa's original desire to move to the beach area did feel good. However, the solution Scott offered in moving back to the area where they had grown up also felt good. Both were making changes in their lives and both followed the way they felt, making changes toward only what *felt* best. Scott compromised within his boundaries, as he offered an alternative in search of something that felt good to him. Lisa compromised within her boundaries, as Scott's idea also felt good to her, so she followed her feelings all the way as well. Both compromised within their boundaries to form a win-win situation! Also, each held integrity toward their Inner Guidance, following their feelings all the way. This left them both *feeling* wonderful towards moving forward with their new lifestyle.

Compromising within each other's boundaries can create an all round good feeling win-win situation!

Remember, as we learned in Christy's camping weekend, when you don't maintain a boundary, you can possibly open a door that causes unnecessary pain to occur. Maintaining your boundaries means following what *feels* good and being true to your Inner Self. Following that feeling of what is best for *you,* so you are always led along a blissful path.

When another has a different desire that doesn't feel so good to us, we know it doesn't feel good for a very good reason. At times, as we can see in Lisa and Scott's story, compromising is inevitable. Scott and Lisa are in a committed relationship. Lisa's desire to move was revealing that she was seeking change or possibly searching for something more. Desires that large don't go away overnight. All desires are initiated at a Soul level and come forward to assist in personal and unified growth. When ignored, they can linger and create distance within the relationship. We can see in Lisa and Scott's joint decision making that compromising within each others boundaries can assist in forming a great solution, and can leave two parties feeling wonderful!

Looking back at Christy and Todd's camping story, Todd could have compromised by suggesting another walk later in the day, or he could have waited and asked one of the other members when they awoke. On the other hand, Christy could have suggested cooking some breakfast together. In compromising within boundaries, it is important to always seek a win-win situation where both parties *feel* happy with the outcome.

There will be times in a situation where there are two or more people seeking different outcomes. Each decision can have an impact on the other. This happens in a committed relationship, such as with Scott and Lisa. It can also happen in a family relationship, where you have a small group living under the same roof. In this situation, decisions arise where compromising is beneficial. Following the way to *feeling* good within joint decision making, while respecting the other parties' feelings and ensuring they are also *feeling* good, will create a great outcome. When two or more parties are unable to jointly form a win-win situation, relative issues may continue to arise, creating other barriers along the way.

It is important to always follow the direction that feels good. It is never a good idea to move toward a direction that feels uneasy. I would not recommend under any circumstances moving toward something that feels uncomfortable. No decision is worth proceeding with to make another happy and yourself miserable. If you are unable to come to a final decision with another and any suggestion they make doesn't *feel* good in that moment, politely let them know that neither one of these alternatives is feeling good. When you let someone know how you are *feeling,* it is then easier for that person to understand your position. At a gut level, we all intuitively know that if something doesn't feel good, there is good reason. If the other person still remains persistent, know you have done your best and soon enough, in their own time of growth and awareness, they will come to understand that you are not responsible for their happiness.

BOUNDARIES VERSUS CONDITIONS

It is important in understanding the difference between boundaries and conditions.

A boundary is something you place for yourself to allow yourself freedom of choice. Boundaries stem from an act of self-love.

A condition is something you place on someone else with the intent to only satisfy Self. A condition, when placed on another in this way, is an act of control.

When we trust our Inner Guidance and are led in a direction by Self, in lieu of a direction requested by another, we have set a boundary. Remember, boundaries are important to protect your own inner happiness and desires. We all require boundaries to ensure we maintain truth to our Inner Guidance. Boundaries allow us to have our own freedom of choice and personal independence.

On the other hand, when we place limitations on another person that affects their personal decisions for Self, then we have set a condition. It is important to understand that conditions are placed in this way when we are feeling distrust in a particular situation. We think that we must place a condition on another to manipulate their choice when we are not receiving, or are not going to be receiving, something from them that will make us happy.

Both boundaries and conditions appear to have a strong impact, though this is misleading. Boundaries are strong as they include a loving energy for Self. A loving energy for Self is a powerful, positive energy. Conditions appear to be strong, whereas in actual fact, they are not strong at all. Conditions placed on another, against their personal choice for Self, are initiated from the energy of fear. Fear is an illusion, it is not real, and therefore it has no true force. Love can override and diminish fear, whereas fear has the ability to override love through focused thought, but it cannot diminish love, for love never dies. Love is the only energy that is eternal.

Boundaries are strong as they include a loving energy for Self.

When you learn that your happiness is derived from within, you will more fully understand the importance of implementing your boundaries. It is then that you will behold the ability to allow yourself to be, do, and have all that you desire. It is then that you are able to offer *yourself* the gift of freedom!

On the other hand, when you learn that happiness is only temporary when deliberately derived from another against their better judgment for Self—and could possibly deplete their happiness for Self—you will more fully understand the negativity of a condition. It is then that you will come to understand the importance of allowing another to be, do, and have all that he or she desires. You will be one who is able to offer *another* the gift of freedom!

BEING TRUE TO YOURSELF

The first step in being true to yourself is owning integrity. Following through on your word. Following through because it is in *your* best interest.

When we make a decision and hold to that decision, it feels good. When we make a decision and back down from that decision, it doesn't feel so good. Prior to making a decision, it is always best to *feel* for the answer. You will make a good healthy decision when it feels right inside. Then, when the time comes to act on your decision, it will be a whole lot easier to follow through because it *felt* right in the first place. And if it felt right in the first place, then it should still feel right today; therefore making it a whole lot easier to have integrity and follow through today.

Being true to yourself relates to following your heart. When you hear your heart speak to you and you follow through, you have integrity toward your own Self. When you have integrity toward your own Self, it is easier to have integrity when the situation at hand involves another.

When we are not being *true* to ourselves, we can create unnecessary pain for ourselves. Let's take a look at an example:

Skye made a decision to purchase a beautiful, new, red BMW. She had never owned a brand new car, so was very excited about buying it. It was a dream she had held for many years. One of Skye's very close friends, Bill, came to visit one evening and Skye excitedly showed him the brochure for her new car. He said to Skye, "Wow, what a marvelous looking car. But I think you should buy the new silver one instead." Skye said, "You know, I really love that red color and I have always wanted to own a red car." Bill replied, "Oh, the silver is much nicer than the red. I have never liked that red color. I would definitely go with the silver if I were you."

Skye was becoming concerned about choosing the red BMW. And after some consideration, she decided the silver was indeed a nice color, so she went along with Bill's suggestion and bought the silver one instead. Skye loved her brand new, silver BMW—until a few weeks later, when she noticed the new, red BMW on the road. A disappointment was growing within as Skye realized she really did love that red color. The more she saw the red BMW on the road, the more she became disappointed. The silver color was nice; however, the red color was the one she had *always* wanted. Skye wished she had listened to her own desire when it came to the color and not to Bill's.

Had Skye gone with her inner desire and chosen the color she loved, she would have enjoyed her new car even more. When Skye trusted another's judgment before her own, she really wasn't being *true* to her own Self. Skye's story shows us how important it is to listen to our own Self speak from within.

Everything you *feel* within is about *you* and what path is best for *you*. When you have integrity and follow the path that is best for yourself, you are better able to emanate happiness along the way. You will feel more giving of yourself. It is a wonderful feeling to give of YOU. Actually, it is the only truth you have to give. All other forms of giving are material based. The most uplifting part of yourself you can offer anyone, is giving freely of your loving energy—your truth from within.

SELF-RESPECT

When we are true to ourselves, by listening to our feelings and following through on our own decisions, we are acting out of self-respect. Every time we give to Self in this way, we strengthen our self-love. Self-respect is an inner strength. We have to maintain an inner strength to be able to follow through on decisions at times, and to do this, we must have self-respect.

Self-respect defines our boundaries. Self-respect actually provides us with the strength we need to implement our boundaries. Self-respect and boundaries both go hand in hand, and both illustrate an emanation of self-love.

Respect for Self initiates the earning of respect from others. In other words, respect for Self is the attraction mechanism for drawing respect from others. It always starts with respect for Self. If we have difficulty respecting Self, then another is also going to have difficulty showing us respect. We need to treat ourselves the way that we wish to be treated. When we treat ourselves a certain way, we are in essence teaching others how to treat us.

In order to *feel* respect for Self, we must like ourself, and we must take care of ourself. We must believe that we deserve to be treated well. We must stand tall and proud and believe in what our inner truth is telling us. Or, in other words, follow our instincts and not back down from that truth. At a gut level, what we *feel* is good for us *will* be good for us. It all comes back to trusting our Inner

Guidance. When we know our Inner Guidance is there to support us and help us toward all of our desires, then we know we have a friend within. This friend within is indeed a true part of who we are at an energy level. As we connect more and more with this inner friend, we will come to understand that we are certainly not alone. It is then that we will begin to believe we are worthy of our every desire. It is then that we will find it easier to respect ourself and follow what feels right, so we may reap the harvest that we deserve!

If you feel that self-respect is lacking in your life, then *ask* to *know* self-respect and *ask* to *feel* self-respect. Make a decision along the way to be kind to yourself and take care of yourself. For when you take care of yourself, you will make sure your needs are met and self-respect at that point is naturally a given. Then simply relax and take pride in your self-respect as it grows and flourishes.

GIVING AND RECEIVING RESPECT

The giving and receiving of respect relates directly to how a person *feels* about him or herself. When a lack of respect for Self or a lack of respect for any other is present, it always stems from a lack of self-love.

We, as adults, initially teach respect based upon our own awareness from what we have learned. When children are young, adults teach them through their own habits how to respect themselves and how to respect the adults. Or, in some cases, how to disrespect themselves and disrespect the adults.

If the adult owns self-respect, the adult will naturally have good boundaries with the child, and the child will quickly learn how to respect the adult. On the other hand, when the adult doesn't have self-respect, the adult's boundaries are repeatedly overstepped and the child learns to disrespect the adult.

Let's take a look at an example of Tayla teaching her children to give and receive respect:

Tayla and her two sons, Bradley and Mathew, went to Disneyland this past summer as a special treat for Bradley's eighth birthday. It was a gorgeous sunny day. They went on so many rides and had a fantastic time. The day began slipping away and soon Tayla realized they had one hour left before they had to leave the park, so they decided to visit Toon Town and the Disney characters in that last hour. Bradley told Mathew he wanted to see Donald Duck. Mathew said that he wanted to see Mickey Mouse. As they approached the Toon Town entrance, they noticed a long line ahead to see Mickey Mouse. They saw yet another long line to see Donald Duck. Tayla told the boys that unfortunately they wouldn't have enough time to see both characters. The boys instantly began to argue over which one to see. Bradley demanded to see Donald Duck; after all it was his birthday. Mathew demanded to see Mickey Mouse because he hadn't seen Mickey Mouse in three years, and Bradley had visited one year ago with his friend and saw Donald Duck then. Tayla saw what was coming and knew that if she didn't take control here, this could quickly get out of hand and create a bad ending to this magical day. Tayla stepped in and made a firm decision. She told the boys the reason they were here at the park was because Bradley had requested this gift for his birthday. She then told Mathew that unfortunately they would not be able to visit Mickey Mouse this time. However, if he were to choose Disneyland when it came time for his birthday and this same type of instance arose, then he could choose his favorite character, or his favorite ride if that were the case. Mathew pouted for a few minutes, but Tayla ignored his pouting and stood behind her decision. By the time they moved through the line and met Donald Duck, Mathew was then feeling much better and the two boys posed together with Donald Duck for a memorable photo.

As we can see in this Disney experience, Tayla stayed strong and followed through on her decision. Due to Tayla's respect for Self, she managed to maintain the boundaries that were required to handle this exercise. During this exercise, the boys were both educated in self-respect by seeing the way in which their Mom dealt with the situation. This taught the boys to not only have respect for their mother, but also taught them how to gain respect for themselves. As the boys become young adults, they will move forward with a clear vision of the importance of self-respect.

Tayla remained calm when speaking to the boys, with a tone of loving strength, while acknowledging and understanding each of the boys' desires. This showed respect for the children. When the adult shows the child respect, the child understands that he is entitled to respect and therefore learns to respect himself.

When the adult doesn't have respect for the child, the child thinks he doesn't deserve respect and therefore learns lack of self-respect. If Tayla had raised her voice, demanded the boys be quiet, and ignored their desires, she would have shown lack of respect for the children, and then each child would have learned lack of respect for others in return. Also, if Tayla had tried to please them both, it could have produced stress for her in leaving the park on time, and revealed a lack of self-respect and boundaries, teaching the boys just that.

Both the giving and the receiving of respect are extremely important in the child learning to initiate healthy boundaries—which promotes a sense of self-love.

I am defining the giving and receiving of respect from a child's point of view because that is where lack of respect is initiated in society. We are trying to teach our children well and are teaching them, for the most part, as we have been taught. However, when many of us were not taught from a place of self-love, how are we able to teach otherwise?

The ill effects we witness, brought about from the lack of respect we have offered another, being a child, a teenager, or even an adult; can be reversed when respect for Self is initiated first and then practiced. When we have respect for Self, we can offer respect and therefore teach respect to others. We must have something in our possession before we can give it away.

We can start by gathering our own self-respect, which comes from being kind, caring, giving, and loving to Self. As we gain self-respect, it naturally implements a new structure into our own lives, then also into our children's and any other that exists within our immediate surroundings. We can make a difference. It all starts with practicing some self-respect. When we have respect for Self, we have the ability to gain respect from others, while offering respect to them at the same time—the giving and receiving of respect!

SELF-KINDNESS

How do you treat yourself? Are you kind to yourself? Do you partake in something that you love at least once a week? Take a moment to ponder how kind you are to yourself, and how often you take time to fulfill those inner desires.

Name two acts of self-kindness you recall this past week that made you feel really good. I am not referring to life's necessities, such as shopping for food or clothes, or a regular workout, for example. These can be more necessities than they are simple pleasures. Any simple pleasure you can think of that you normally would not need, or have to do for yourself, to physically survive. You may have taken a stroll in the park by yourself, played the guitar, visited the spa, or bought yourself some flowers. It doesn't matter how small it seems, or how large.

Were you able to recall two acts of self-kindness? If you had difficulty recalling two acts of self-kindness, then take a moment to consider the *desires* of self-kindness that have been missing in your life and what you can do to change that. The kinder you become toward Self, the kinder the energy becomes all around. Self-focus through positive, loving eyes releases energy of just that. Others will feel the loving energy we emanate and be drawn to reciprocate with the same.

Don't seek to forget yourself...be selfish enough to remember yourself!

Finding Self-Love

EMANATING THE HAPPINESS

Don't you think it's time to treat Self lovingly by implementing your boundaries, owning self-respect, being true to yourself, and making yourself happy? Implementing these attributes is a golden key in finding and then owning *self-love.*

The best thing we can do for any other person is to create our own inner happiness. When we haven't given much time and loving energy to ourselves, we tend to feel that we don't have much energy to offer any other. We feel spent as many of us will say. Meaning, we have exerted all our energy into other areas—to other individuals, or other endeavors. When we feel spent, we feel like relaxing and taking it easy. This is our Soul *guiding* us to take care of ourselves, to relax and rejuvenate. When we do grant ourselves time to relax, we are in that moment *giving* to Self and are refilling our cup of energy. When we don't do this for ourselves and continue to give and give, we can become quite overwhelmed and begin to lose a part of who we truly are, meaning our *self-love.*

Fulfill Self and you will naturally emanate happiness to others!

Begin today by filling yourself up with all the happiness you have been depriving yourself of. Practice acts of self-kindness often. Nurture your self-love. Then go about your life joyously, always seeking those things that make YOU happy, and you will naturally emanate that uplifting energy to your loved ones and to the world!

Part 2

KEYS TO
YOUR CREATIVE
POTENTIAL

***

*A selfish act from the heart is not what we keep
but what we give to ourselves so we might
have something to give away...*

Chapter 4

Let's Get Creative

HMMM, HE CREATED US IN HIS IMAGE

Within the realm of our Universe exists a magnificent, loving energy, which flows all around us and through each and every one of us. This magnificent, loving energy I am referring to has over the years been referred to as God, All-That-Is, Universal Energy, etc. I like to call this loving energy that exists everywhere *God-Love-Energy*. So as not to create any confusion when we refer to it in this book, we will refer to it as *God-Love-Energy, All-That-Is,* or *Universal Energy,* depending on the topic at hand.

For many years of my life, I never quite knew how I felt about the term "God." However, I felt in my heart there was truly more to life than I could visibly see in my surroundings. It wasn't until I began to learn about the loving energy through which I create, and my Soul that assists me to create, that I started to connect all the pieces.

For me personally, I like and use the term, *God-Love-Energy*, as this term seems to suit the feeling I get about the loving energy all around me. I don't think it matters what you call this life force of energy, as long as you are able to connect to and become aware of this *Positive Loving Energy* that exists all around. Find a term that feels best to you, so you can relate in your own way.

At a Soul level, we are all connected to and a part of this same life force of God-Love-Energy. It has been said that at the beginning of time, a division occurred—where God divided into a multitude of like energies, each one being named a Soul—each Soul representing an extension of his own energy, and each Soul representing an expression of his love. This dates back to the biblical understanding that "God created us in his image." Therefore, we each are connected to the same likeness of energy—the God-Love-Energy—giving us equal ability with which to create. The big message here is we can create with love, thus creating a life of happiness, laughter, joy, passion, etc. Or, we can create without love, thus creating a life of pain, frustration, anger, jealousy, etc.

We are all creators, and we all hold the same power with which to create. We are each equally able to be, do, or have anything that we *desire* in this world. However, for many of us, our understanding of our power to create has unfortunately been lost over time. I would like to help you to not only get to know *you* at a Soul level, but would also like to help you find those golden keys that will allow you to be the creator that you came here to be!

In this section, we are going to focus on our creative energy, and learn how to adapt a complete understanding of our create ability into our awareness, which will then allow us to be, do, and have all that we desire.

Let's Get Creative

When we are connected to our Soul, we are then connected to this powerful source of God-Love-Energy that exists everywhere. We have then accessed the magnetic power of our creative Universe and our creative potential is totally available, and totally unlimited!

CREATIVE ENERGY—LIKE ATTRACTS LIKE

Back in Australia, I worked for a large bank for many years. This was long before I began to discover the golden keys to my creative awareness. It was a very busy bank with a front line of around twelve tellers. I mostly worked in the back office of foreign finance, though sometimes, when it got quite busy, I would also work the front counter.

Each day, I shared lunch with a sweet girl, Leanne, who worked the front counter full-time. One day at lunch, Leanne told me of a reoccurring nightmare she was having almost every night. She explained to me that in each nightmare she was being held-up at gunpoint by a bank robber. I was really surprised and told Leanne that I was having a similar nightmare. Each day, we would meet for lunch, and each day, we would share the same story about being held-up. We would discuss it and scare ourselves silly. This went on almost daily for a number of weeks. I recall feeling very scared thinking about the nightmares and the thought of being held-up. It was around six weeks before the nightmares stopped. The day the nightmares stopped was a day I have not forgotten. I was helping out one day on the front teller line and Leanne was working next to me. I had just finished serving a customer, when a colleague, Johnny, called out to me from the other end of the office. I closed the box with the money in it and went to see what this friend needed. As I was talking to Johnny, all of a sudden, there was an extremely loud bang as the bulletproof, protection screens shot up to the ceiling. Even though we did a security check every morning, this bang was not one you ever get used to. It was frightening each time it was set off. We all looked around and no one said anything, so we all thought it was a false alarm. A minute or so later, after the initial shock of the loud bang had worn off, everyone began to laugh. Then all of a sudden, Fiona, another teller, went running to Leanne. Fiona had been held-up once before and knew that the blank look on Leanne's face was that of utter shock, most likely from being held-up. Fiona was right. Leanne had been held-up and was the one who had set off the bulletproof screens. Unfortunately, the bad news is the shock and pain Leanne incurred from that experience. The good news is no one was physically hurt; the robber escaped with no money and was caught on film.

The robber apparently had not joined the line of customers waiting to be served. Instead, Leanne noticed him walk up and wait directly behind the customers that we were serving at the time. Right as my customer left is when Johnny had called me to the other end of the office. The robber then waited for Leanne to finish with her customer. It is interesting to note that Johnny called me in that very instant where it could have been me serving the robber in lieu of Leanne. Also, there were around twelve tellers working at that same time. How was it that Leanne and I happened to be working side by side and both of us had been having the same nightmares? Leanne and I actually dismissed it at the time as some weird psychic encounter, as neither of us had ever witnessed anything like that before. We felt that somehow we had both been given prior psychic knowledge through our dream state of this particular event.

To sum it up today, yes, we were provided with a type of psychic awareness through our dream state. But this awareness we were receiving was actually a warning message being delivered by our Soul, telling us that our fearful thoughts from that day were attracting what we were focusing on—a hold-up!

During our daily lunch discussions, I am sure we both were having strong warning gut feelings while we were discussing our dreams and the scary thoughts of being held-up. Looking back, I was one who did not usually flinch at my guidance system warning me to stop miscreating. I had absolutely no idea at the time that my fearful thoughts were negative. I also had no idea the bad feelings that I was feeling inside were related to my disconnecting from my Soul, due to me focusing on something so negative. At that point, I never even considered that I had a Soul who existed within me and was helping me.

Due to the fact that I had been ignoring my guidance during the day, my Soul then tried to get my attention through my sleeping state in the form of a nightmare. My Soul was repeating my daily thoughts back to me during my sleep through the nightmare. That is precisely what a nightmare is. (We will cover "receiving through our dream state" in more detail later in this book.)

First, due to Leanne's and my continual emanation of fear-based energy, we both attracted this unfortunate event. Our fear was feeding off each other, as we discussed and mulled over the thought of being held-up on almost a daily basis.

Second, we were forewarned continually by our Inner Guidance, due to the fact that while we were discussing the thought of a hold-up, we were feeling scared like crazy. Well, I know I was. *(Feeling really scared and tortured within is a feeling of disconnection!)* Then each nightmare was being repeated, as we were each day miscreating the same thing, so each night our Soul would warn us once again!

Third, we manifested it quite well in the world of co-creation. Without our fear intact, the robber had no energy to move toward. We invited him, or in other words, attracted him, through our fearful state of energy. His energy did not line up with any other teller in the bank. His energy lined up with the energy of Leanne and me. The possibility that he ended up being served by Leanne instead of me could be that her energy lined up to match his just that much more than mine. However, to be standing next to her and to have almost served him instead meant that I was very close to her with my like energy.

Let's look back at these three steps above. First, we initiated the process of miscreating through our fearful thoughts. Second, we were not allowing ourselves to be led by our Soul, due to the fact that we ignored our Inner Guidance—meaning we did not *let the fearful thoughts go*. Continuing to think fearful thoughts and miscreate caused the fear we were emanating to attract the like energy of the robber. Third...BOOM! Miscreation received in form of manifestation.

Let's Get Creative

These are the three simple steps in creation:

1. Think - Thought initiates creation
2. Follow - Follow the feelings from your Soul
3. Receive - Receive manifestation

For each and every action, there is an equal and opposite reaction. So true! As a robber thinks of robbing a bank, he attracts the person who thinks of being robbed. The statement, *"fear hits us in the face"* is very correct. When we fear something, we are in fact inviting it into our surroundings. Remember, fear is actually a negative expression, which the victim (in this case, the teller) is *feeling*. The teller's fear attracts the negative minded, fear-based energy of the bank robber. Two fear-based, negative energies coming from opposite mindsets are then lining right up! The robber is very aware of what he is conjuring within the negative mindset, which is an extremely fearful attempt at becoming very rich. Unfortunately, the bank teller is not so aware, as he or she does not understand they are creating from a negative, fear-based mindset. Or miscreating, we could say, as the teller surely would not be deliberately creating this if only he or she knew better. The outcome being: two similar, fear-based energies of opposite mindsets (but focused on a similar outcome) attracting toward one another—the fear of robbing the bank versus the fear of not being robbed. The co-creation attraction process is this: both have the same thoughts of robbing (though from opposite ends of the story, still the thoughts are of robbing), and both parties are emanating extensive amounts of fear.

It doesn't mean if we think once of being robbed that we will be receiving that manifestation. To manifest something that large and impacting requires quite an amount of ongoing energy focus, like the fearful energy I continually delivered leading up to the bank hold-up. The amount of focus I delivered prior to the hold-up taking place was many weeks of daily continual focus.

Continual, extensive, focused thought is required to attract a major manifestation.

Do not be concerned over your previous thoughts if you believe they were thoughts that were miscreating. Whether they are from the past minutes, days, weeks, or months, you would need to have placed quite a considerable amount of thought into a larger, more uncommon manifestation for it to occur. Even then, if it is a miscreation, your Soul knows that and will do all that it possibly can to steer you away from actually facing the manifestation. All you need to do today is follow your Inner Guidance—in other words, *pay attention* to your *Soul* each step of the way. If you have been afraid of something occurring, simply let go of any relative thoughts each time they pop back into your mind.

It is *so* important to take notice of what we are focusing on and how we are feeling in each moment. To determine your creative power, work at paying close attention to what you are thinking about throughout the day. Then pay close attention to what you are receiving in the following days and weeks. As we have discussed, every single thought has creative potential. However, it takes a certain amount of energy, accompanying a certain type of thought, to determine if and when a manifestation will take place.

Let's Get Creative

As you pay more attention to what you are focusing on, and then to what you are receiving in the following days, weeks, and months, is when you will come to understand the focused energy required to attract a minor or major manifestation. A minor manifestation is something more likely to occur that wouldn't be surprising and requires little focused thought for it to manifest; whereas a major manifestation is something uncommon that happens on a rare occasion and may be surprising when it does. Much focused thought is required for a major manifestation to occur. Each time we offer focused thought, we are aligning the energy one step closer to the receiving of the manifestation. It takes time to align our energy with the energy of a larger manifestation, as the larger manifestation includes energy that we are not so accustomed to knowing. We align energy easily to what we *know* and have *felt*. When the energy has been aligned previously to a major manifestation—meaning we have received that major manifestation—it is then easier to align the energy once again to receive a similar, major manifestation. At that point, not as much focus is required, as we can more easily find the old *aligned feeling* place of *owning* the manifestation.

A manifestation is not something that must be seen, or in other words, it is not something that is only material. A manifestation is any form of witnessed outcome brought about from focused attention. It can be anything non-material—for example, a conversation—to anything that is material—for example, a dream home. Any form of event, circumstance, item, or living thing is a manifestation. Manifestations are formed energy. Manifestations are everywhere, just as energy is everywhere.

After gaining a better understanding of how we create through our thoughts, we now know the importance of paying closer attention to what we are thinking as we go about our day. The story of the bank hold-up offered us a close-up view of how continual, fearful thoughts can be destructive in our lives. If we have the power to create like that through fear, just imagine the power we have to create like that through love!

When we focus with continual, loving, passionate energy toward any desire that we hold, by the creative, magnetic power invested within us and within the Universe all around us, the manifestation must occur.

For the most part, we attract a situation based on a similar previous thought pattern. However, it is possible to attract a negative or a positive situation based on a similar wavelength, or in other words, a similar frequency that we are *feeling* at the time. For example, we may have had a bad day, with a chain of continual, unfolding, negative events. We are traveling on the road, cursing at other drivers, stressed out and disconnected, when in the next moment, we become involved in a car wreck, or we get pulled over for speeding. The thought of a motor accident or speeding ticket may not have been in our previous thought pattern at all. However, our negative, disconnected state, in that moment, attracted a negative situation to occur. For example, we may be feeling slightly angry with someone and then stub our toe on the corner of the doorway. The frequency of our disconnected state, in the moment, will determine the frequency of the negative situation that we attract. On the other hand, the frequency of the connected state, in the moment, will determine the frequency of the positive situation that we attract.

Negative energy mingles with negative energy. Positive energy mingles with positive energy. For the most part, I have found that manifestations line up for me based on my previous focused thought. However, on rare occasions, I have found that a manifestation occurs when I do not recall offering focused thought to the subject at hand. On these occasions, I can clearly see each time how my energy lined up with the energy I am mingling with.

WE CREATE THROUGH LOVE OR FEAR

As we go about our day, we have a choice to create with one of two different energy types. We have a choice to create with *love* or *fear*. As we focus with fearful thoughts, we are in that moment attracting negative situations. As we focus with loving thoughts, we are in that moment attracting positive situations.

We are expressionists. We are creators. We create through our expressions of love or fear.

We are offering a creative energy every time we apply *focus* to a particular object or situation. We can apply focus either with a low energy, or we can apply focus with a high energy. Or, we can say we apply focus with a negative energy, or a positive energy. Or, yet again, we can say we apply focus with a fear energy, or a love energy.

Once we discontinue focus on a particular subject, we are no longer offering our creative energy. Though, if enough focus was previously applied, the manifestation might still occur. Once again, we are always being led. If we are following our guidance from our Soul, we will be led toward a desired manifestation, and we will be led away from an undesired manifestation.

Happiness, excitement, joy, passion, and laughter, for example, are all expressions of *love,* or in other words, positive expressions. Anger, misery, judgment, complaining, and worry, for example, are all expressions of *fear,* or in other words, negative expressions. In each moment, we always have a choice...*love or fear.*

Expressions of love can invite wonderful, exciting things into our life. Expressions of fear can invite unwanted, undesirable things into our life. The choice is ours. Nobody else is choosing for us. Our expressions in each moment reveal who we *are* and define who we are *becoming.*

BEING LED

Every time we offer a focused thought, we receive guidance in the form of a feeling from our Soul. When we think an uplifting thought, we feel great. When we think a painful thought, we don't feel great.

We are able to fully connect with our Soul when we are in alignment with its same energy, that of a positive, loving energy. We disconnect from our Soul when we are not in alignment with our Soul's same energy, which is when we are thinking a thought of lesser energy, or negative energy, that the Soul can't align with. This is when our Soul naturally cannot connect, so it naturally begins to disconnect, and we don't feel good inside. This is how our Soul offers guidance to us; it is connecting

Let's Get Creative

when we offer good thoughts, or it begins disconnecting when we offer lesser thoughts. It is important to realize that it is not the Soul that initiates the disconnection. It is the physical part that initiates disconnection due to the physical not aligning with the *same* energy of the Soul— that of *positive, loving energy.* Our Soul is always available 24/7. It is always the *thought* that initiates connection or disconnection.

Every time we get a feeling from within, we instinctively know the answer to what we were just thinking. If it was a positive thought, we will receive a positive feeling. If it was a negative thought, we will receive a negative feeling. We just need to be listening *within.* We do know what's best for ourselves, and another knows best for themselves. We each have our very own guidance system intact with every answer we could ever need.

Our feelings are designed to lead us in the best direction. If the feeling is a pleasant feeling, we are moving toward something that will uplift us. If the feeling is an unpleasant feeling, we are moving toward something that will not uplift us. Each feeling that is pleasant or unpleasant holds attractive magnetizing energy; so each time we receive a feeling, we are also in creative or miscreative mode. In our connected state, we are in a loving state, so we are attracting loving situations. The more connected we are on a regular basis, the more love we are attracting into our lives. In our disconnected state, we are in a fearful state, so we are attracting negative situations. The more disconnected we are on a regular basis, the more negative situations we are attracting into our lives.

When we listen and allow ourselves to be led by our feelings from our Soul, we will stay on our path of happiness and will know what doors to open and what doors not to open.

IT'S TIME TO GET CREATIVE

We create from our point of connectedness.

We miscreate from our point of disconnectedness.

As we watch ourselves creating or miscreating through our power of thought, we will begin to notice those manifestations appearing before our eyes. It is then we will *feel* and *know* that we truly are creators.

So, what are we waiting for, it's time to get creative! Take a pen and paper and list three desires you would like to see manifest within the next twelve months.

Next—imagine it is twelve months from now and these three desires have each manifested. What do they *feel* like? What do they smell like, sound like, and look like? Use all your senses to envision each manifestation. Then describe in words what it feels like to have each manifestation in your life today.

Pretending the desired manifestation has already hatched helps us to truly *feel* what it would be like to have it in our life. As we find the *feeling* place of already owning the manifestation, we are in that moment creating it into existence.

As you pay more attention to your thoughts and feelings and to your daily unfolding of manifestations, no matter how large or how small, you will begin to notice just how powerful your thoughts and feelings truly are. We are basically creating our future from each and every moment, through our thoughts and our feelings.

Are you starting to comprehend the *power* of your thoughts? Can you see how important it is to pay attention to your *focused thoughts?*

Are you starting to comprehend the *power* of your feelings? Can you see how important it is to pay attention to your *feelings?*

Work at deliberately focusing on the life you would like to create. Pay attention to your thoughts, releasing the ones that don't feel so good, and spend more time focusing on and milking the ones that do feel good.

We will cover a topic in the next chapter on visualization, a technique where you will learn how to spend quality time focusing on and attracting *desired* manifestations.

CO-CREATING

When two people are involved in sharing, they have come together due to a previous alignment of thoughts and feelings. They have a common identity of desires.

In relationships, we co-create each time we share interaction of any kind. It may be a home we have bought together, an apartment we rent together, or it may be choosing furniture together. All sharing in any shape or form is manifested through a co-creation process.

Co-creation from two or more individuals has the ability to offer energy unlike a creation by one person. When two or more people share a passion for a similar interest, the energy shared can offer spirals of positive energies, reaching a height of passion that can only exist through a co-creation process. It is exciting to have a personal goal, but to share a similar goal with another and co-create that into existence can be extraordinary. Two minds coming together to create under the same topic, within the same timeframe, launches additional energy than that of a single creator. This is the reason why mass consciousness is understood as having a powerful impact.

A co-created manifestation can also occur from a negative input. Two or more people can receive something they did not desire and be in the same place at the same time, brought about from a common fear, a common complaint, etc. The bank hold-up story I shared with you earlier in this chapter is a great example of two or more people co-creating in this way.

When we are not in a relationship and seeking a mate to co-create with, it is important to first *feel* good about ourselves. The way we *feel* about *ourselves* will determine the type of mate we will attract. For example, if we are feeling down most days because we dislike our job, or have been arguing continually with a family member, or just complaining about life in general, then our point of attraction will be from a place of feeling miserable. In this place, we are only able to attract another who is also feeling discomfort within his or her life. When two people come together feeling negative, then the relationship, for the most part, will start out negative.

It is important to get ourselves to a place where our job is uplifting, we feel great most days, we smile much of the time, and life is pretty good. For then, we will naturally attract a like-minded person. When two people come together already feeling great, then the relationship, for the most part, will start out great.

Sharing, I feel, is one of the most beautiful aspects of a relationship—sharing dreams and desires with a loved one and watching manifestations unfold together—whether it be making love, or making a home. To create together through passionate energy is an ultimate state of being. When you feel good about you and then naturally attract another who feels good about him or herself, the co-creation experience can be magical. You have the ability to continue to feel wonderful, as you each feed off of the wholeness of the other. Each of you understand what it takes to feel good about oneself, so endeavor to maintain your own positions of giving to Self, through acts of self-kindness. As you each continue to fulfill Self, you will fill your own cups and have wholeness to offer. What goes around comes around. What a wonderful, exciting way to co-create!

SEEING THE PATH WITH CLARITY

We came here to create. We also came here to co-create.

As we understand our part in this creative process, we will begin to understand the power we behold. Gaining *clarity* is a golden key to becoming a powerful creator and co-creator. We must *know* to become. When we understand our abilities to be, do, and have, we understand our reason for *being.*

Being clear on who we are, where we came from, what we do, where we are going, and how to get there, is necessary in understanding the concept of life itself. If we are not clear on these aspects, how can we possibly be the powerful creators that we came here to be? It is simple: we cannot *deliberately* create to our full capacity when we are not *clear* on our own identity and make-up.

When clarity is ours, we have the ability to manifest and bring to life our every desire!

Ask to have clarity in your ability to create. *Ask* to see your path with clarity. Clarity opens doors. Clarity sets the stage. When clarity is ours, we easily move beyond what is, and move toward what path is rightfully ours. We become fully aware of our own presence and value. Awareness sets us free. Our awareness manifests into the true connected state of Body and Soul. We become one with Self—and we become one with All-That-Is.

Chapter 5

Ask and You Shall Receive

THE POWER IN THE ASKING

When we wish, pray, desire, or hope for something—for anything in our lives—we are simply *asking*. For some of us, we have been fortunate enough to gather some faith in our asking. For the rest of us, we tend to wonder why we hope or why we even pray at times; and we question the possibility that someone might even be listening.

When we come to understand more fully the power of love within our magnetic and energetically charged Universe, we can then understand why it is that every time we ask, we are being heard. God-Love-Energy exists everywhere and through everything. It is what exists at the basis of all *desired* creation. It is transmitted within each and every one of us at birth. No individual is different when it comes to our connectional birthright to God-Love-Energy. Manifested within us, we each have the power to tap into the unlimited potential that God-Love-Energy provides.

To tap into our unlimited potential, we only need to *ask* with *desire*. We can ask in a variety of ways. For example, we ask when we visualize, pray, daydream, ponder, wonder, imagine, or simply by voicing a desire out loud. Any form of focused thought involves some form of asking. Each time we ask, the asking is released from our physical in the form of energy. This energy attracts to it like energy. As energy comes together, it forms and molds. With more like energy coming in, brought about from more focus, it forms and molds again until a manifestation is produced. The more energy released from focused attention, the more likely the manifestation will occur.

Focused thought produces energy, which produces manifestations.

All manifestations are a make-up of energy and are continually becoming. Even after we receive a manifestation, the manifestation still continues to take new shape and form over periods of time. This aspect of becoming and changing within each manifestation over time is directly related to the changes within our asking, which is directly related to the changes in our thought patterns. As our asking changes over a period of time, it changes the energy put toward the manifestation. As the manifestation is formed from energy, the manifestation must change to align with the new thought pattern of asking.

As we go about our day, it is important to pay attention to the way we word our asking. If we say, "I want to see positive activity around me today," then that is coming from a loving energy. If we say, "I don't want to see negative energy today," then that is coming from a fearful energy. Take a moment and *feel* the difference between these two energies. The energy is basically emanating from the key words. The key words in the first statement are "positive activity." Therefore, we are focusing on the positive activity. The key words in the second statement are "negative energy." Therefore, we are focusing on the negative energy. We may be wishing to be rid of the negative energy, though the point of focus is still placed on the negative energy. We are always attracting to us via our focused attention.

It is very important to take notice of how you imply the asking. Take notice of the way you *feel* as you are asking. Your feelings will always let you know if you are asking from a loving place, or from a fearful place. We have ignored these feelings for so long, we don't even recognize their existence most of the time; especially when we are focusing on a minor manifestation, then our feelings are subtler, but they are definitely present. It is a matter of simply *desiring to notice* them again. The more you notice them, the stronger they will appear to be. They are actually not really getting any stronger, they were always this way, you are just now more *aware* of their presence.

Isn't it a wonderful feeling to know we are *never* alone? Each time I receive, I am amazed to this day that I am that important to be heard, also that I am loved by some other force that I never knew existed. Now I know it has been there all along, is truly a part of me, and is linked to the God-Love-Energy that exists *everywhere!*

We can ask for anything we desire, such as a car, a new job, happiness, peace, or a vacation. Or, we can simply ask to know the answer to something that intrigues us. It is important to realize that our Soul is there to assist us in finding our way. It will lead us toward all of our dreams and goals. Feelings from our Soul guide us within each step and within every decision along the way.

We receive in a variety of ways. For example, we can receive through our gut feelings, our meditation, and even our dream state. We are receiving when ideas are popping into our head. The receiving of new information that pops into our head from out of nowhere is directly linked to our Universal connection with *All-That-Is*. Each time we have one of those things we call a brain wave, it is actually our Soul sending through the answer to a question we had previously asked. It is a *Soul wave!*

We are all receiving from our Soul when we don't even realize it, with sudden desires, sudden impulses, and sudden ideas popping into our head. We can receive at any minute of any day, no matter who is around us, or what we are doing. It is when we are in our *connected* state with our Soul that we are readily able to receive all Universal knowledge.

We are all creative creatures and we are all intuitive creatures. We are imbedded with our own righteous power to explore and then to create all that we desire. We are not alone. We have guidance every step of the way. We only have to *ask* and then be *aware.*

When you feel a dream surface from within and would love to see it manifest into your existence, simply *ask.* There is trueness in asking. I have found it personally. I ask and I receive each day of my life. If you can have *faith* in that statement and implement it into your life, you will feel your Soul, your best friend, with you the whole way. Asking with *faith* is a golden key in the world of creativity. We can receive all of our dreams when we ask with *faith*. Have faith in that!

Faith is indeed an important element in the creative process. We must *let go* and have *faith* if we are to receive. Faith is our ability to let go and trust in the power of Universal Energy.

When we have faith in our stride, we'll have manifestations by our side!

We each hold the exact same ability to create. We are all part of the same. We are all part of All-That-Is. Begin today, by becoming aware of your connection with your Soul, to ensure you are creating from your best possible stance. Keep asking along the way and keep an eye on your asking. Is it coming from a place of love, or from a place of fear?

Love and create…or fear and miscreate!

IT IS OKAY TO "ASK"

When we hear a dream—a desire, deep in our heart—it is always okay to ask for that dream. We are all here for the same reason. We have all come from the same place and we are all going to the same place. Each person deserves as equally as the next.

It is important to follow our dreams. When we follow our dreams, we are on track and are heading in a great direction.

Your Soul delivers your desires from within. In your quietest moments, when you are able to fully receive and when you least expect it, your Soul will send gentle nudges, impulses, and insights to lead you toward passions and desires that will assist in keeping you on your pre-desired path to happiness. Your Soul knows each person and each circumstance that will assist in getting you to your desired manifestations. Your Soul knows your pre-desired path—your path to a higher awareness—and always knows the best steps to take from here.

When you feel a dream within, it is okay to *ask* for that very dream. How many times do you hear people say, "I had that dream my whole life but never followed it," or "I always wanted to play the violin," or "I always wanted to dance like that." Sad, isn't it, when you think of all the unfulfilled dreams out there?

We are here to grow, not to be stagnant. There is an ever-abundant supply of creations just ready to be launched. Each time we ask, we set more wheels in motion within the Universe. Our magnetically charged Universe is always at work. Our asking is always *heard.* The desire will become ours when the *faith* is ours that we will receive.

We are here to imagine and create...and then go beyond what we have already created!

When we realize our thoughts are creative, it becomes clear that our thoughts are creating the abundant supply. We then realize that we can *ask* for anything we desire. When we go beyond current thought, we then go beyond current existence of matter. Each time we *ask,* we move forward. We are growing and becoming.

We came here to be creators! So it really is okay to ASK!

Ask and You Shall Receive

ASKING IS PRAYING

When we ask with desire, we release energy, which attracts like energy.

When we visualize with desire, we release energy, which attracts like energy.

When we pray with desire, we release energy, which attracts like energy.

When Jesus said, "Ask and you shall receive," I believe these above statements are an example of what he meant.

When we are praying, we are simply asking.

The only difference in each expression of asking is the time spent in focusing on the desire, and the amount of passionate energy put forward while focusing. Prayer and visualization are really not so far apart. They are both sittings that require quiet surroundings. Also, both usually involve an extended time placed aside with focus on wishes or desires. The more time spent praying or visualizing, the more creative energy we are sending out. Prayer and visualization are both a powerful form of asking. (Appreciation is also an extension of prayer, which we will discuss later in this book.)

We can see why biblical times taught man to pray. It is an excellent form of asking. Also, due to the fact that many people have a strong belief in prayer, they emit a considerable amount of faith.

When you wish to manifest something into your life, whether it is a home, a car, love, happiness, a trip, or whatever it might be, you can simply use any form of asking you desire. Whether you choose prayer, visualizing, daydreaming, or just simply asking in your mind as you go about your day, it all works. However, the most powerful form of asking is always extended time placed aside as in prayer or visualization.

When you wish for a loved one to get better; pray, visualize, and/or ask as you go about your day to see your loved one in good health. It is true that each person can only create for themselves through their own power of thoughts and feelings. However, you may influence their outcome by seeing them in the positive light that you know they would wish for themselves. As you see them in a positive light and not in pain, you will be evoking the best energy possible from them, which does influence their feelings in that moment as you draw from them any love that may be present.

THE ART OF VISUALIZATION

Visualization is an art in creating our existence as we desire it to be. A visualization sitting consists of extended time placed aside; in order to deliberately direct our thoughts toward circumstances, events, or material items that we are wishing to attract into our lives. Around fifteen to twenty minutes is a good amount of time to place aside for visualization.

A visualization sitting is best conducted in the morning before we start our day; for this is when we are fresh, well rested, and connected. Visualizing in the morning also sets us up for the day with a positive outlook. It gets us on the right foot as we walk out the door. If morning doesn't work and afternoon or evening is better, we can still accomplish our outcome. However, later in the day, we may need another five moments to assist in reconnecting with our Soul. As we go about our day, we can get caught up in trying or stressful moments. These moments cause us to disconnect from time to time throughout the day. The later in the day, the more time we may need to reconnect, depending on how we are feeling at that time. We may have had a wonderful day with fewer disconnections, so we may be feeling pretty good and ready to jump right into it.

Our aim in visualization is to place ourselves in the perfect creating mode. The perfect creating mode is a connected state between our Body and Soul. When we are feeling good and are also feeling relaxed within, we can easily hold a positive energy within our body that maintains a link with our Soul. This provides not only a clear, precise vision for creating, but also a stance for reaching a high, passionate, creative energy. It is a good idea to turn off outside influences, such as televisions and telephones, so that we may have free time and not be disturbed.

To begin your visualization exercise, choose a position to sit, either on the floor or in a comfortable chair. If you are feeling good within, you are ready to begin visualizing. If you are feeling tense or uncomfortable within, spend a few moments and focus on your breathing, in order to release any lingering uncomfortable thoughts. You also might find that connection comes easier with some light meditation music in the background.

When you are feeling relaxed and connected, it is then time to focus on your desires and begin creating. Choose the first item on your list that you desire to manifest into your existence. For example, it might be a new job, a new home, a loving family environment, or a brighter bank account.

Let's pretend you start with your family and your wish is to *feel* peace and love around your family. Begin by seeing your family around you enjoying your company and each other's company. Visualize having great times together. Feel the peace and love around you. Continue to see this encounter for a few minutes, and *feel* the good energy between you and your family members.

Next, let's say you are wishing for a new job. Begin by seeing yourself already in this new position. *Feel* how wonderful it is to arrive at this new job each morning. See yourself going about your day attending to your new duties. See the positive aspects in this new role. Take a few minutes to really *feel* yourself in this new position.

Continue to visualize each desire until you are finished. If you managed to find a powerful connection place while visualizing, you may experience a lightheaded feeling for a moment or so when finished. Take a moment to get your feet on the ground, so to speak.

The first time you visualize your desire and it appears out of reach or not so accessible, that's okay. Most new desires at first don't *feel* they are within reach. That is because energy vibrates on different levels. It can feel slightly odd when you first visualize a desire that is not within your reach; as the energy you are *reaching for* is not in alignment with the energy you are currently *feeling* in relation to that desire. The essence of our work here is to match our frequency of energy with the same vibrational frequency of that certain object of desire. In spending this quiet time, we are in fact changing the vibrational frequency of our energy to match the same energy of the desire we are asking for.

As we visualize our desire again and again, we begin to feel the desire become more natural, due to the fact that each time we visualize, we are aligning our energy one step closer to that desire. Each time we visualize, our frequency of energy is aligning one step closer with the same frequency of the manifestation. The desire starts to *feel* like it is becoming a part of who we are, as we are now vibrating on a closer wavelength. Soon we feel as though we can almost reach out and touch the manifestation. At this point, we *know* that we can have the manifestation. We finally *feel* that we deserve it. We can actually feel the shift that has occurred within. That shift has enabled our energy to match the energy of the manifestation.

VISUALIZING WITH COLORS

Color visualizing is a wonderful tool, but not a must. It is an additional outlet that assists in aligning our energy with the *feeling* place we are wishing to find. You may wish to include color visualizing each time you visualize, or you may wish to include it once a week, or once in a while. Decide how you *feel* at each sitting whether or not you would like to include color visualizing.

When you are choosing a color, pick a color that *feels* good to you. (A color chart and descriptions are provided under the next sub-heading.) You will find that each time you visualize, you may have a desire to use a different color. *Trust* the color that *feels* right to you each time. The color that you choose will assist in providing you with how you are seeking to *feel* that day.

First, see the color you have selected. Then see the color, as an extension of bright, colored energy, flow smoothly and lovingly down from the Universe and enter at the top of your head. Breathe deeply, and with each breath, see the color flow through each part of your body. As the color moves through you, *feel* the positive influence the color provides. For example, if you have chosen blue, *feel* the peace and harmony the color blue is providing as it moves through each part of your body. See the color blue reach every part of you and feel the sensations of this color within you. Then see the color leave your body, exiting at your toes. As it leaves, *feel* the wonderful sensations that color has provided. *Feel* the difference within your body.

PALETTE OF COLORS

When you are ready to begin your visualization, choose the color that *feels* right at that moment. The warmer the colors that you choose, such as red, orange, or yellow, the more passion you are seeking in your day. The cooler the colors that you choose, such as blue or green, the more peace you are seeking in your day.

You can also pick and send any of these colors to assist someone in need of upliftment. Send pink to someone you are wishing to offer love to. Send white to assist in healing. Send blue as an offering of peace. Send the color with *feeling*. See your loved one receiving the color and the loving influence the color provides as it moves through their body. See them *feeling* the effect of the color. Then see your loved one in the way you know they wish to be seen.

Here is an example and definition of colors you may choose:

RED: Passion. Strength. Grounding. Influencing others. Red provides strength to assist in going forth with greater confidence and ease. The color red can assist when you are to perform on stage or speak at a seminar, for example.

BLUE: Peace. Harmony. Searching for balance. If you are feeling highly strung that day or feeling stress in any way, blue can help you feel grounded, while placing you in a more peaceful frame of mind.

PINK: Close relationships. Romance. Loved ones. Heart bonding. Choose this color for a deep, sweet taste of love. Pink provides for longing of the heart. It fulfills our passionate lusting for romance and desire. Use this color whenever you feel lonely, lost, or longing for love in your life.

LILAC: Unconditional love. Harmonious love. Loved ones. Trusting. Openness. Bonding. All-is-well. When you are seeking a harmonious love link with your family or friends, use lilac to feel the peaceful bonding of love. Lilac can also assist when you require an open trust to develop in any relationship.

ORANGE: A passionate color. Provides for warmth and understanding. Helps to amplify your outgoing side. Choose orange when you require passion with flare, or when you are searching for that inner energy that makes you want to dance and feel free. Use orange to also assist in situations that require your social skills to be strong and effective.

YELLOW: Wisdom. Encouragement. Hope. When we are writing an essay or taking an exam, for example; yellow feeds our wisdom, giving us the will to follow through and complete. When you are in need of guidance, some wisdom, and a friendly hand, feel yellow and be led to success.

GREEN: A peaceful color. Brings us close to nature. Supplies balance of earthly energies. Use green to promote a peaceful balance with our earthly physical plane. Or to supplement the body as vitamins and minerals do.

WHITE: Heavenly upliftment. Promotes well-being. Unconditional love. Choose white when you are feeling ill, in pain, or simply in need of some loving care and upliftment. Focus on certain areas that require loving energy, such as arthritis or a leg injury, and supply it with a pampering of heavenly white.

GOLD: Angelic support. A connection to All-That-Is. A color for bonding to life itself. Use gold when you are searching for Spiritual knowledge and require guidance and support from other sources of Spiritual helpers. *Ask* for help and guidance when needed. Know that you will receive what you open your vision to—angelic guidance is always there to support us and help us on our way.

LETTING GO, LETTING GOD

Once we have deliberately asked for something we desire, then to receive it, we must step aside and let *God-Love-Energy* do its work. In order to receive all desired manifestations, we are required to *let go and let God.*

When we have faith, we naturally let go. This letting go creates a free-flowing energy, thus allowing all of our desires to easily flow to us.

When we let go, we relax into a free-flowing energy.

When we push and try to make things happen, or if we worry and think we are not going to receive something, we are putting up a negative wall of energy, thus blocking the manifestation from free-flowing to us. Manifestations can only free-flow to us via a positive wave of energy. When we are emanating any type of negative energy—for example, worry or frustration—we are disconnecting from our lifeline, due to the fact that each of these energies are fear-based energies. As we have already discussed, negative, fear-based energy disconnects us from our Soul and from our loving link to God-Love-Energy.

Letting go is a very important factor in the equation of creation. Thus, the reason for the term, *let go, let God.* When we let go, we are letting the *God-Love-Energy* in. We are surrendering. We give up the trying, pushing, or shoving. We give up the negative energy. At that point, when we give up the negative energy, we naturally connect to the positive force of God-Love-Energy and all desired manifestations can free-flow to us.

When we sleep, we reach a pure, natural, connected state. This would best describe the meaning of fully letting go. As we drift to sleep, all negative energy is released from our body.

It is important to let go of ill thoughts that pop into our head. As soon as you receive an ill thought, work at letting it go. Our thinking habits are our beliefs, which make up who we are. Something that we hold on to is something that makes up who we are.

If you are having trouble sleeping, now you know why. Maybe you are hanging on to lesser thoughts from that day and not letting them go. As soon as you *let go* of lesser thoughts, such as worry, concern, and frustration, you should drift off to sleep quite easily.

The reason so many people spend time in meditation is to reach a pure, natural state that feels so good, like the relaxed state we reach in our sleep. We do this in meditation by releasing thought. We release the thought during our waking state—that's what meditation is. Meditation is a great tool to assist us in reaching an aware, deliberate state of letting go, and then letting God.

When we say let go, let God, in essence we are saying let go of negative energy and allow the natural God-Love-Energy to flow through us.

Negative energy is a dense energy, which depletes our ability to connect with our life force—our Soul. Become aware of energies you carry around. Are they light or heavy energies? Do you feel good or do you feel bad? Pay attention to the way you are feeling. When you are not feeling wonderful in the moment, then let go and reconnect to your life force—your Soul. No outer influence is worth disconnecting yourself from feeling absolutely wonderful!

In each step, we can simply ask...then be led...and have faith...then let go...and let God!

I received the story within the following poem through meditation when I was in the early stages of questioning my Soul and my connectedness to All-That-Is. Upon completing the meditation, I immediately received this poem. I would like to share it with you.

A Loving Invitation

I feel an inner strength that I've never felt before,
It takes me to new heights and I see an open door.
I know not to push it, I feel that deep inside;
Allow it to just be and soon it'll open wide.
I see it open inch by inch as time passes by,
I stand and peek through and know soon I'll understand why.
Then one day I get a feeling, "Hey look at the door,"
It's open very wide now; I wonder when I'll explore.
I get another feeling and gently this is how it went...
"Do you want to go now? You are ready to advent."
I start to get excited as I float up from the ground,
I get a feeling in my back; it's wings I see I've found.
I can feel them start to flutter as I move on through the door;
This new world is so beautiful, and then there's even more...
A way to describe it would be like Alice's Wonderland;
Natural beauty boasting definition and clarity in each stand.
I think I'll be an angel with these new wings I have found,
But something said inside, you're a butterfly that's abound.
I'm feeling very beautiful as I flutter through the air,
Then I said, "Okay what's over here that wasn't over there?"
This feeling pulsed my body, though words cannot be found...
"God is here" this feeling said and I sensed he was all around.
My blood a rush, I knew right then why this had to be;
I invited God into my world...and now he's invited me!

I want to point out that when writing this poem I never knew what the word "advent" meant. The word "advent" just came to me, so I trusted and went with it. I looked it up in the dictionary after finishing the poem.

The meaning as described on www.dictionary.com:

<u>Advent</u>

1. The coming or arrival, especially of something extremely important:
    a. The liturgical period preceding Christmas, beginning in Western churches on the fourth Sunday before Christmas and in Eastern churches in mid-November, and observed by many Christians as a season of prayer, fasting, and penitence.
    b. <u>Christianity.</u> The coming of Jesus at the Incarnation.

This totally surprised me when I realized the word "advent" was linked to a biblical understanding. It offered me confirmation that I truly was receiving this poem/information from a source other than my brain, due to the fact that my brain did not store knowledge of the word "advent." "You are ready to advent" I believe meant that I was about to become enlightened and truly connected to the positive force of God-Love-Energy. Something else I found interesting is that I, at first, decided to be an angel, but then *felt* I was a butterfly. When I look back at the poem, it makes sense that I was a butterfly. A butterfly undertakes a major transformation from that of a caterpillar to its final form. I didn't realize at the time, however, I really was going through a major transformation myself.

The receiving of this poem is a moment in time I will never forget. I remember it so clearly. What a wonderful way to learn. It showed me that meditation could indeed assist in quieting my mind for information to be received from my Soul and its connected state to God-Love-Energy.

RECEIVING MANIFESTATION

When we have visualized our desire to a place of *feeling* aligned to it—in other words, matching the energy of the desire—the hatching of it then feels like the next logical step. We usually receive our desire when we are in a place of *knowing* that we are about to receive it. Can you recall that feeling when you expect your desire is around the corner? That feeling when you *know* that it is about to happen?

These are the formal steps in receiving our desired manifestation:

1. <u>Ask</u> - Ask for your desire in any way that you choose, through visualization, prayer, daydreaming, or just plain simple asking at any point throughout the day.

2. <u>Align</u> - Align your energy. As little as five minutes of passionate focus is all that is required each day for each desire, until you are aligned. You will feel your energy shift as you become more aligned with your desire. You will know when the manifestation is aligned, as receiving it will *feel* like the next likely step.

3. <u>Be Led</u> - Pay attention to your Soul and follow what *feels* best. Listen and be led.

4. <u>Expect</u> - Learn to have trust in receiving. Expect that you could see this manifestation appear at any time. Don't look too hard for the manifestation. Looking too hard promotes a struggling energy, which in fact is a disconnecting energy. We want to stay connected here so we can be led.

5. <u>Receive</u> - Reap the rewards! You deliberately focused your passionate attention to set the creative wheels in motion. You then allowed yourself to feel good enough to stay connected. And you followed your inner feelings, your Soul's signals, all the way. Take responsibility for being a fabulous creator!

Remember to act in this order:

1. Ask
2. Align
3. Be Led
4. Expect
5. Receive

At times, we receive a manifestation that it is not quite the way we had hoped it would be. If the manifestation shows up and doesn't feel right, or is not quite as you had hoped for, be prepared to wait it out. A closer match or possibly even an exact match can occur. Sometimes, we receive close matches along the way and feel very happy with what we have received. Listen to the way that you *feel* and you can never go wrong. Your feelings will let you know if there is something greater out there well worth waiting for.

My friend, Kenny, shared this story with me. Kenny worked for an advertising company on the East Coast. He had been dreaming and visualizing for some time of

94

becoming the General Manager of this company. One morning, Kenny arrived at the office to discover that he had been promoted to the position of General Manager, just as he had dreamed. However, there was only one slight problem: the position was at their office on the West Coast. Although Kenny had also dreamed of living on the West Coast one day, possibly when he retired, he knew that at the present time, uprooting his two children from their school was something that he and his wife, Mary, would not feel comfortable doing. He was saddened to turn down the position, but he remained confident that the right position in the right place would turn out.

In the following weeks, Kenny fine-tuned his visualizing and made sure he visualized the position happening on the East Coast.

Two months later, Kenny arrived at his office one morning, and was excited to hear that he had been awarded a promotion to Chief General Manager at the East Coast office! Kenny could not wait to tell Mary of his promotion.

Not only did Kenny wait and receive the position at the location of his choice, but he also received a higher paid position as Chief General Manager. Kenny smiled to himself. He had been visualizing more money coming in, however, he had not anticipated where it would come from—he had left that part up to the Universe!

Those who believe in their dreams will live their dreams!

Many years ago, when I was living in London, I was offered a position within a small bank as Personal Assistant, assisting the General Manager in overseeing a staff of twenty-five. The salary was roughly £300 ($600) per week. My roommate told me that this was very good money and recommended I take the job. At the time, I had some large bills coming due, and I had virtually no savings in the bank, so I wanted to increase my salary as much as I could to assist in covering these bills. I knew it was indeed risky, however, I had a *feeling* that I could be paid more, so I turned down the position. My roommate was shocked and told me that she would have taken the position, as ones like that didn't come available every day.

I *felt* deep down that if I kept my focus on my original desire, in lieu of fearing what might never be, I would then stand a good chance of receiving a closer match to my desire. I spent some time visualizing. I saw myself receiving the salary that I intended on getting. I saw and enjoyed the *feeling* of the dollars in the bank. I ignored outside influence and maintained my focus. Then only one week later, I received a call offering me a position as Personal Assistant to the General Manager, assisting in overseeing a staff of more than two hundred. I was to be awarded a salary of £400 ($800) per week. I was thrilled. However, it didn't stop there. This particular job required extra long hours, due to recruitment measures from a shortage of staff. Soon I was working seventy-hour weeks, which at the time totally suited my lifestyle. My salary increased to £700 ($1,400) per week!

It is *so* important to trust in ourselves. We really do have the answers within. When we *feel* that something is not quite right, then it can be in our best interest, each and every time, to take a risk and wait for our *true desire* to manifest.

MISCREATIVE ENERGY

Throughout the day, when we are not paying attention to our focus, we can actually be miscreating and not even realize we are doing it. For many of us, when we are feeling in a negative state, we don't acknowledge it due to the fact that we have been taught to ignore our emotions. When we look around us, then express what we don't like, we are in that moment *asking* for more of what we don't like.

Many of us are miscreating every day of our lives. We see something that annoys us and we complain about it. We talk about it to others, we mull over it, and then our magnetically charged Universe automatically sends a similar energy right on back to us. Then we complain some more to another that listens and we miscreate something similar again. *Complaining* is jam-packed full of miscreative energy. Each time we complain, we get nothing but negative energy boomeranging right on back to us!

As you work at maintaining a positive energy, it may be slightly frustrating as you find just how often deluding thoughts may enter your mind. Before you know it, you are off and running with these deluding thoughts, speaking of all the things that are not going to bring you what you truly want! However, don't despair; simply *ask* to be more *aware* of your thoughts. Then, trust that soon you will be in control of your thoughts, thus smoothing your path to enriching manifestations.

Pay attention to your thoughts as often as you can. At first, it may not be that simple; however, after some time passes of deliberate intent, you will soon create a natural habit of becoming instantly aware of what you are focusing on. Once you begin to acknowledge that your thoughts are indeed *creative,* you will naturally *desire* to pay more attention to them. Whether you are thinking positive, uplifting thoughts, or whether you are thinking thoughts that are miscreative, once you are *aware* of their magnetic power, you will simply *desire* to become more *aware* of their presence.

Each day as your life unfolds before your eyes, pay attention to each small manifestation that occurs, even a conversation that you hold with someone. It may be a happy manifestation or one that doesn't feel so good. Next, search back through your thought pattern from the previous days and weeks. If you have been continually paying attention to your thought pattern, you will find relative thoughts that have now manifested into this time and place.

As you pay more and more attention to your thoughts, it will become easier to recall your thought patterns. A friend I know, Jeanie, had quite the argument with a lady at the local grocery store. She walked away very annoyed and told a few friends about it, and then a few more. Instead of letting go of the argument, she held on to it and let it really bother her. She explained to me how she didn't want to feel this way anymore, and how she wished that others would be a whole lot easier to get along with. I asked her if she could recall any other recent arguments she had encountered with different individuals. Jeanie said, "Oh yeah, you know I did have an argument with the mailman the other day. He keeps putting junk mail in our mailbox, when we have asked him many times not to do that. He knows it really bothers me."

When we find it hard to let go of something that bothers us, we *hold on* to that negative energy, allowing it to become part of our energy. Each time we think about an argument and mull over how much it bothers us, there has to be an inner gut feeling present. A gut feeling that includes warning feelings, letting us know of our miscreative energy present. Meaning, that after a previous argument, we held on to those negative thoughts and ignored those negative feelings, which then assisted in creating yet another argument to be attracted into our presence. After ignoring these warning feelings for so long, they have now become almost unnoticeable. To get ourselves to a place of *feeling* really good most of the time, we want to become more *aware* of these warning gut feelings that are present each time we are miscreating.

Try to take notice during the day of your feelings. When you are miscreating, your Inner Self will let you know with a negative feeling. Once again, we are taught to ignore our feelings, so get yourself back into a mode of listening to the way that you *feel. Ask* to be more *aware* of your feelings.

When you pay attention to your feelings and pick up each time on the negative feeling inside, you will know to stop what you are focusing on, and instead, refocus your attention to another object—one of desire. As you continue to implement this into your life, you will be pleasantly surprised at how much brighter your days become. You will notice the smaller, annoying things leave your existence, and will begin to see more uplifting aspects appearing in your life.

We have a vast contrast in this world, ranging from extremely negative conditions to extremely positive conditions. The choice is ours. What are you wishing to attract into your life? Negative attracts more negative. Positive attracts more positive.

As you begin to focus more on positive conditions, watch as more positive conditions appear in your life and implement themselves into your every day. Watch your life turn around. The more you focus on positive conditions, the more your life will continue to uplift.

Soon you will start to ignore the negative conditions that were once controlling your life, as you will not have time for all the pettiness that exists there. Instead, you will move into a richly fulfilled environment of rewarding, positive aspects and outcomes.

Ask to look beyond, or rise above, the petty things that exist around you. *Ask* today to witness more uplifting expressions in and around your life. *Ask* to have pleasant conversations. *Ask* to see more positive aspects in others.

How often do you feel down or uncomfortable? Do you wish to change the way that you *feel* most days? Life is meant to be fun and uplifting. We have freedom of choice in each step—to create or miscreate!

We are so free in each moment, we are even free to miscreate if that is our choice!

It is all a matter of choice. The more you look toward a positive attitude in your everyday life, the more you will receive just that. As you move into your new day with a new aligned, positive thought pattern, you will begin to notice more positive energy around you. In the beginning, there may also be some old, unwanted energy that arises here and there. For it will take time, usually a few weeks, for the previously miscreated energy to leave your existence. Though, the better it gets, the better it gets. It is worth your time and effort. The power is in your hands. You are a creator—and *you* are in the driver's seat the whole way!

LETTING GO OF THE SMALL STUFF

When we let go of the small stuff, we make room to receive.

The above statement can be true in regards to material items, or it can be true in regards to thoughts in our mind. When we let go of material items that we no longer need, we make room for other items to manifest into our existence. The same goes for thoughts in our mind. When we let go of negative thoughts, we then make room for positive thoughts to come through. When we clear useless stuff from our lives, we feel wonderful. We feel a sense of room to move. We feel a sense of freedom around us.

It is a great idea to remove items from your home that you no longer need and have become clutter. For where there is room, there can be improvement. And with improvement, comes growth. Also, when we let go, or in other words, release items, we open the door and make room for Universal Energy to deliver other freshly desired manifestations.

We feel a sense of freedom within when we clear out old energy. Items can take up space around us. Even though we aren't really aware, the crowding of energy does weigh heavy on the way that we *feel*. If you haven't cleared out the closet in the last year, then it is time for some energy cleansing. The same goes for the storage room, the garage, and any other room you can think of that is a little crowded. Make yourself an appointment this weekend and give your home and surroundings some good old cleansing. While you are doing that, you will be giving *yourself* some good old energy cleansing.

The less cluttered your mind, the more room to receive clearly from your Inner Guidance. As you become more aware of lesser thoughts that serve no purpose, you will become more aware of releasing them. As you release them, you will feel a harmonizing feeling within. This feeling is a stronger and clearer *connection state* to your Soul and to All-That-Is. Before, when we hung on to lesser energy, it didn't feel so uplifting, as lesser energy drags us down and feels heavy. As we release the lesser energy that serves no purpose, we feel much lighter in each step.

Work at clearing your energy in and around you. It is a wonderful gift you can give to yourself. Let go of the lesser stuff and make room for the real stuff!

CREATING MINOR MANIFESTATIONS VERSUS MAJOR MANIFESTATIONS

Many of us are quite good at passionately visualizing our desire. However, many of us cut off the receiving of our desire because we are not feeling worthy of receiving it. For most of us, it takes steps of smaller manifestations to reach our worthy state of believing that we can have the larger manifestation.

Anything we can imagine with our mind's eye, we can create. We each behold the ability to create anything that we feel worthy of, or in other words, anything that we feel we deserve. If it can be *felt,* it can exist. We are all able to create equally.

Any one of us is worthy of any manifestation that we can imagine!

When we take an Olympian from the 1960's and compare his or her time results with an Olympian of today, in many instances, the results differ greatly. However, when we compare the results from one event to the next event, we see that they have grown at a steady rate. The reason for this might be that their belief pattern was not able to accommodate such an increased margin at the next Olympic event. However, a portion of improvement was believable. Then, with each event thereafter, another portion of improvement was believable, and then another portion. When an athlete increases the margin considerably at one event, it could mean that this athlete holds a higher rate of belief in him or herself, thus providing the ability to increase the margins in the results more considerably.

When we understand the only difference in each manifestation is our *passion* and *faith* put forward, we then know that the size and value of the manifestation has no significance. When it comes to minor and major manifestations, we can look back and realize the difference in receiving each one is only a factor of time. It is the alignment of energy and faith that requires time. When we ask, Universal Energy will deliver in the correct time and space, depending on our clarity and the passionate energy we have placed toward our manifestation. The more clarity we hold and the more passionate energy we offer, the faster we can align and then the faster our desire can appear.

If we can only slightly grasp our worthiness as creators we can create amazing results!

So what are we waiting for? We can manifest all of our desires when we are feeling worthy! Feeling *worthy* is a golden key, which enables us to receive. The power is in our hands, each and every step along the way.

Learn to have faith in your own creative power and in the magnetically aligning power of the Universe. Know what you want and *know* you can have it. We are here to create. Ask for it. Align to it. Be led to it. Expect it. Receive it. Then enjoy it. You are *so* worthy. You are a creator!

Enlightening material I recommend that offers insight regarding our overall existence, as well as our relationship with God, are the wonderful books, *Conversations with God* and *Friendship with God* by Neale Donald Walsch. For information visit: www.nealedonaldwalsch.com

Chapter 6

Reprogramming Thoughts and Fine-Tuning Feelings

SOCIETY PROGRAMMING

Many of us, over the years, have been taught to ignore inner emotions produced by our Inner Guidance. As a result, we have learned to compromise by listening to others' advice before our own. When we are led by outer forces in lieu of our Inner Guidance, we move blindly toward creating our own existence. When this happens, we are *allowing* others to program our thoughts toward our daily creativity patterns, in lieu of doing it ourselves.

We don't have to allow our thoughts to be programmed by outer forces in society. We have every right to program our own thoughts and therefore our own experiences. We also have the *power* to program our own experiences. We have been fighting forever and a day to gain the self-control we feel we are missing. So now it is time to step up. It is time to pay attention to our own Self, to infuse our own control, and to rediscover our own personal power. We can allow *outer influences* to mold who we are becoming, or we can utilize *our* own power and orchestrate *our* own future.

We can begin today, by allowing others in society to orchestrate their own energy patterns, while we train ourselves to orchestrate our own energy patterns. It is time to turn within and pay attention to our very own thoughts and feelings. We can retrain our thoughts, which will in turn bring about positive feelings, which will *recreate* our energy make-up, which will then create the person that we *desire* to be.

RETRAINING OUR AWARENESS

Every focused thought we offer today is creating who we become tomorrow. Every focused thought is important if we wish to *feel* good tomorrow. If we wish to feel good tomorrow, we need to make sure our thoughts are productive today. So now we are going to review our thoughts, and then reprogram our thoughts, in order to develop a new thought process, which will allow us to nourish ourselves with a fresh, positive outlook. To begin, we must train ourselves to become very *aware* of what we are thinking.

Pick two people that are in your life today. The first person you choose will be someone you don't always get along so well with, or you may not feel so good in his or her presence. The next person you choose will be a person you really adore, someone that makes you feel wonderful almost every time you are together. Take a moment to ponder why you feel the way that you *feel* in each individual's presence—what buttons they push, or what love strings they pull.

Okay, so now let's take a look at the feelings that each of these two people *evoke* from you. Do you notice a vast difference in the way you *feel* toward each person? Let me tell you something very interesting. The way that another person thinks and feels can influence the way that we think and feel. Yes, they can. The way that another emanates their energy—or in other words, the way that another is *feeling*—has influential magnetizing energy that attracts and directly evokes similar *feelings* from us. But the big point here is: *Only if we allow it to!*

And the second big point is: *We are creators, we receive what we give focus to, so if we are seeing negative energy, then how did that negative energy get in our face in the first place?* Because we offered attention toward a similar negative energy type last week, or last month, and didn't *let it go* when we could have. It is a boomerang effect. When the negative energy is launched and coming at us, we have the choice at that moment to rise above the negative energy and to let it go, or we can walk away and complain. Next time you walk away and get ready to do some complaining, try and recall this following statement—complaining throws a boomerang that always returns to hit the complainer in the head!

To make this easy, we will name the person you chose that brings out the best in you the *Love String Puller*. The person you have chosen that does not bring out the best in you; we will name the *Button Pusher*.

Ah, the Love String Puller, if only the world was full of these! The only problem is that if the world were full of Love String Pullers we would not have the Button Pushers to mirror our mistakes! Yes, the Button Pushers actually mirror back to us any negative energy we have been previously emanating. This negative energy we have previously sent out may have been directly related to this Button Pusher that's in our face today, or it may have been related to a different Button Pusher. I guarantee you though, if you have one Button Pusher in your environment much of the time, then there are more! They may not be in the exact same environment, but you may have one at work, one in the family, and one within a group of friends. If you are emanating and therefore attracting lesser energy often, you will be attracting any Button Pushers that may be near. As soon as you walk away and complain about a Button Pusher, you may as well grab a microphone and say, "All Button Pushers, please come and push my buttons!"

It is nice to know that we have the Love String Pullers that mirror that other wonderful side of us isn't it? Well, we *can* invite more of those Love String Pullers into our lives. And believe it or not, we can assist in turning the Button Pushers around to become Love String Pullers during *our* interactions with them. For each person, at a Soul level, is made up of pure, positive, loving energy. We just have to learn to see through any lesser energy to the loving energy underneath.

We are responsible in every instance for our own thoughts and feelings. However, it is also important to understand how others can influence us. When we understand how another can influence us, we can then use this knowledge to assist us in reprogramming both our reactions and our general habit of thought.

When we reprogram our way of thinking, we can make a huge difference in our lives. I am not saying that we will be perfectly happy and blissful forever and a day, but we can get awfully close! When it comes to the way that we interact with others, we do have a choice. We can have mature interactions, or we can have immature interactions. When we choose love, we choose maturity. When we choose lesser, negative energy, we choose immaturity. Being mature doesn't mean we can't have fun. Maturity includes the best child-like fun there is! Maturity includes positive, loving, carefree energy. All that is required is to be as goofy, carefree, fun-filled, and childlike as we wish to be!

Work at letting go and rising above negative energy. You will find that as you turn the other cheek again and again, the negative energy that was once a more dominant part of your life will begin to dissipate, thus playing a minimal role in your life.

Soon you will witness more Love String Pullers and fewer Button Pushers in all of your surroundings. In other words, soon you will be pulling on more love strings and pushing less buttons, therefore magnetizing similar responses from all those around you!

So, the plan is to become fully developed, ripened, enriched, and nourished with mature, love string pulling energy. To do this, we say good-bye to worthless, negative, immature, button pushing energy. And a big hello to our Soul who can now join us more completely on this earthly joyride!

PAYING ATTENTION TO OUR THOUGHTS

It is not easy, all of a sudden, to begin to watch your thought pattern. I know this is a process to work on. I have been working with this process and I know that it doesn't happen overnight. That is why we have *feelings* to assist us in paying attention to our thoughts. Our feelings always let us know what we are thinking in any given moment. When we *feel* that inner warning gut feeling beginning to grow within, it is important to try to take notice immediately of what we are focusing on.

When we don't pay attention to our thoughts, our thoughts can be scattered, unintentional, and miscreating.

Retraining our thoughts takes time, but as we begin to align to new thought patterns that are uplifting and freeing, we will witness a new growth pattern and find true happiness becoming our strength day-by-day. We will then learn to take responsibility for our own creations, each and every one of them.

I catch myself now, mostly at the beginning of my thought process, and have learned to let go and refocus on brighter, more positive thoughts. It has worked for me and I am fine-tuning it day-by-day. The shift of energy I feel within my body has been a miraculous change for me. The choice was mine and I made that choice. It is work; however, if we truly wish to find that balanced happy state that we all have access to, then it is well worth the effort.

When we do pay attention to our thoughts, we place ourselves in the driver's seat and become the deliberate creators that we are meant to be. It is then that we are able to create with clarity. It is then that we become intentional creators with the ability to manifest all focused *desires*.

Our thoughts are extremely powerful. Our thoughts are magnetic. So how important is it to pay attention to your thoughts? If happiness is important to you, then deliberately watching your thoughts and aligning them with positive energy will bring all the happiness you desire!

Ask to replace old thought patterns with fresh, positive, aligned thoughts. Then remind yourself each day to watch your thought patterns. Say to yourself, "My thoughts today create my tomorrow." You will soon find that the more you work with this, the easier it will become.

Tomorrow's happiness rests in the power of today's thoughts!

PAYING ATTENTION TO OUR FEELINGS

Our feelings speak to us on a variety of levels. We receive feelings that let us know if our thoughts are in alignment or not in alignment with our dreams or goals. We also receive feelings that tell us what and when we need to eat and drink. We receive feelings that tell us when our bodies are tired and need sleep. Which clothes we wear best. Which is the best road to take. Who we enjoy being around. What type of touch we prefer. The more we get in touch with the feelings our Soul provides us with, the more in touch we get with our own body and all our own desires.

When we pay attention to our feelings, we know what we are thinking. If we are feeling good, we know we are thinking positive, aligned thoughts. If we are not feeling good, we know we are not thinking positive, aligned thoughts.

Feeling always follows thought!

If you are in the habit of not paying attention to the way that you feel, then you are definitely not alone. The good news is you are able to change that habit. For many of us, we have been taught to ignore our feelings. So to catch our thoughts through our feelings is kind of like a double-edged sword. However, the more we take notice of our feelings, the easier it will be to take notice of our thought process and vice-versa. It is our awareness of "all of it" that is missing. We need to be aware of both.

I began by trying to pay attention to my thought process. Then I tried to pay attention to my feelings. But I realized, as time went by, that I wasn't really paying too much attention to either. My former habits of not paying attention were quite embedded and so were not prone to shift too easily. I was still unintentionally miscreating all over the place. So, I started to *ask* to pay attention to my thought patterns. I also *asked* to be more aware of my feelings.

It wasn't long before I started to become more aware of my thoughts and feelings. As time went by, I became more and more aware of them. Then anything that was important enough, I was starting to catch as soon as the first thought entered my mind. I recall a couple of occasions around this same time when I didn't catch the thought right away. That is when my feelings would step in to let me know I was in that moment miscreating. This is when I realized my feelings had somehow become more intense. To be able to explain this is not so easy, though it was sort of like this—I had to become more aware of one in order to become more aware of the other. In our natural process of creating, our awareness of *all of it* is important if we are to manifest all our desires.

Today, I pay much more attention to my thoughts than I ever did. Also, my feelings are more definite than they ever were. I feel that if you *ask,* as I did, then be easy on yourself, this will all unfold naturally. We have been taught for so long to do all this differently. For most of us, the habits have become quite imbedded along the way. Now it's time to undo what has been done. It is time to release the lesser energies that serve no purpose. And it is time to move beyond our limited beliefs and move toward our ultimate existence!

Ask to become more aware of your feelings.

Ask to become more aware of your thoughts.

Many of us have come to believe that we need to take action to control outer situations. When we let go of trying so hard, or struggling to control situations within and around us, our physical body relaxes and then our Soul can better connect and offer us pure guidance. The more we relax, the easier it is to *feel* our way and be *led* toward what we are looking for.

We are led via the feelings that we receive from our Soul. Our Soul knows what is best for us in each step we take. When our minds are quiet, we can hear what our Soul is trying to tell us. Our Soul is forever providing us with all the clarity we require. We only need to rest our thoughts and listen.

LETTING GO OF LESSER THOUGHTS

Let go, let God and *turn the other cheek* are biblical references, which mean, turn away from negativity and turn toward the Light—toward All-That-Is. As we make a decision to look the other way, it is important that we offer *no* judgment while doing so. It is easy enough to look the other way from something that is lesser energy, but for many of us, we have a good look and then continue to think about it as we turn away.

Another's energy that *they* emanate is always about them. The energy *we* emanate is always about us. When we point the finger at another, we might as well be pointing it at ourselves. As we point, we are in that moment *asking*. The judgments we offer any other do in fact reflect the true way we *feel* about ourselves.

Any thought we think reflects our own love for Self.

Lesser thoughts are thoughts that serve no purpose. They are negative thoughts that do not offer growth. When you notice that another's thoughts or your own thoughts are lesser than pleasant, uplifting thoughts, simply turn your attention away from those thoughts, focusing your attention instead toward thoughts that are beneficial to your own growth and happiness.

You will begin to notice the warning gut feelings inside of you when you get off track and become negative. Let go of those initial thoughts that were obviously miscreating and realign with new positive thoughts. Then appreciate those warning gut feelings for giving you guidance in time of need.

We always have a choice. When a thought pops in our head, the choice is ours whether to play with that thought and create with it, or just simply let that thought go. As we become more aware of lesser thoughts and let them go, we will find in time that lesser thoughts will cross our mind less frequently. The more we continue to let go of lesser thoughts, the more power we will feel toward our choice for growth.

Letting go of lesser thoughts also relates to letting go of any measure of fear, such as fear of illness, fear of an accident, or even fear of being overweight. As soon as you feel fear rising within, it is a miscreative energy. It is cutting off your connection to the all-important Source Energy, or in other words, God-Love-Energy, which rejuvenates, heals, and enables free-flowing, loving energy to circulate through every part of your being. Fear energy disables God-Love-Energy from freely flowing.

A number of years ago in Sydney, I was visiting a good friend of mine, Gayle. During my visit, I showed Gayle some small, but very noticeable, skin blemishes that had appeared on both of my hands weeks before. These skin blemishes were basically scattered across the top of both hands. I had been to my doctor, who had provided me with every available treatment. These blemishes were still very noticeable and the fact that they were not going away really frustrated me. I showed them to Gayle and explained my frustration. Gayle took a look and said, "Why don't you just ignore them, pretend they are no longer there, and see what happens." It seemed like a good idea. After all, nothing else had worked, so what did I have to lose.

I went about my life and ignored these skin blemishes. I stopped focusing on my hands. If I did stop to look at them, I would quickly turn away and not mull over them. I ceased using the medications that I had been given. I just simply forgot about them.

About one week later, I was talking to a friend and was pointing at something when I noticed my hands. The blemishes were completely gone! The only marks left were minor abrasions from the treatment the doctor had used, which were barely noticeable. Unbelievable!

I excitedly paid a visit to Gayle and said, "I am amazed, how did you know this works? And by the way, how does it work?" She just shrugged her shoulders, like it was no big deal and said, "I've been told to do this in the past and it worked for me. I don't know why, it just works." Back then I had no idea of the power of thoughts and feelings. I just walked away shaking my head in wonderment. It wasn't until some years later, when I was introduced to the material from "Abraham-Hicks Publications," that it all came together. I looked back and recalled this story and was amazed. Gayle gave me a huge gift—thank you Gayle! And lucky for me, I was vulnerable and open enough to run with it!

Letting go of lesser thoughts enables us to move on from yesterday, cease negative judgment, and release expressions of fear. It allows us to be the person we wish to be, while living a more exciting, productive, and fulfilling life. Above all, it provides us with the ability to offer unconditional love to ourselves and to all those around us.

POINT OF FOCUS

It is our focus that is imperative to our awareness. One little thought is really not so creative. It is when we are applying *continual focus* that the thought becomes creative. Continual, focused thought is creative. As we add more focused thought, we are adding emotion through the way that we are feeling, which adds to the creative energy. That is why it is wonderful if you can catch your initial thought when it is launched, as, at that point, there is little or no creative energy put forth.

When we focus on something, we are applying an attraction process.

Our awareness level determines where our sensitivity and perception areas lie, due to our focused behavior. When we are sensitive to noise—for example, the barking dog next door—it is revealing that our awareness level is turned up, brought about from recent focus on outside noise. We are simply drawn to what annoys us, due to our awareness level being sensitive to it. Generally, we might not be so sensitive to a particular noise. However, the attention toward it has caused the sensitivity. When we simply *let go* of the issue of the barking dog, we remove our focus. The less focus we apply, the less aware of his behavior we will be. The dog either stops barking, or we simply don't notice the barking any more.

The more we focus, the more we attract. The more we desire, the more we attract. Or, the more we fear, the more we attract. Whatever type of expression we use, we are in attracting mode. All we need to offer is a *point of focus* to set about the attraction process. The length of our point of focus and the amount of emotion we have added determines our power of magnetism. A smaller amount of emotion will supply only a smaller amount of magnetism. The more emotion we apply, the stronger the magnetism.

Our point of focus is our creative point.

Contrast is vital to our everyday choice. Contrast includes positive and negative surroundings. As we see the contrast that surrounds us and survey it, we feel these vastly different energies. To know what we *do* want evolves from knowing what we *don't* want. However, we don't want to focus our energy too long on what we don't want. We can easily view and then turn the other cheek from all that doesn't feel right—to face all that does feel right.

For example, when we are shopping for that right suit or dress, we generally sift through the suits or dresses in the store until we find one that holds our interest. We wouldn't stop at each item, however, and cross-examine it. That would be a waste of time. The way we search for that right suit or dress is a great example of the way we could search through the contrast that surrounds us in our everyday life. We could view and then include, or we could view and then exclude. We could do this instead of stopping and applying judgment, which would save time and energy. We can then redirect this energy toward other areas of interest that deserve our time and energy.

Another example would be when we choose from a smorgasbord of food. We take what we like and generally don't give too much attention to what we don't choose. We wouldn't stand there at the counter and complain about what is left on the shelf—the spinach or the asparagus that we did not choose. Imagine what a waste of time that would be and how it would make us feel. Though, in everyday life choices, we have been conditioned to do just that. We have been taught to readily apply judgment or criticism, which in turn means we are not agreeing with another's decisions for Self or allowing them the freedom to choose—which *also* means that we are including that vibration in our *asking;* thus attracting more of that *same* vibration into *our* own lives.

As we sift through our surroundings in everyday life, we have the ability to choose as we would choose from the smorgasbord of food. I call this the *Smorgasbord of Life.* As we admire people, items, circumstances, and events that surround us, we are in that moment choosing from our smorgasbord of daily choices. What we admire—or in other words choose—we are applying focus to, and therefore including in our vibrational tone of asking. As we see something that doesn't interest us and we remove our attention with no judgment, it does not get included in our vibrational tone of asking. Choose and choose well from the *Smorgasbord of Life* is my motto!

The focus we apply to our surroundings is the focus that creates our tomorrow. Next time you stop to pass judgment on something, ask yourself, "Is this something I desire to see in my life again tomorrow?" If not, then switch your focus to something that is deserved of your time and attention—something you would like to recreate more of tomorrow!

Our *point of focus* is extremely important. When we realize this, we can learn to pay attention to how and where we are applying our point of focus. Every time you find your attention fixed on something of interest, listen to your feelings to see if they are saying yes or no. If you are feeling relaxed or uplifted within, you are in positive creation mode. If you are feeling tense or uneasy within, you are in negative miscreation mode.

The more focus you apply, the more creative power you are sending out. The more energy placed on that same subject over a particular period of time, the more the energy compounds and assists in forming the manifestation.

All matter is energy compressed and compounded. Your continual focus determines this. Focus creates energy, which creates matter.

When we understand the power of our *focus,* we will understand the importance of paying attention. Paying attention to our continual *point of focus* is a golden key in becoming a master at creating an extraordinary life. We are creators. We attract as we focus. All *focus* attracts outcomes, as we reach out and receive, touch and taste, and then continually choose from this exciting *Smorgasbord of Life!*

Chapter 7

Living in the Here and Now

NO REGRETS FOR YESTERDAY

We all have experiences from the past that can leave us daunted and at times pained. Forgiveness is so important. When we forgive others, we are in essence forgiving ourselves. On the other hand, when we judge another, we are in essence judging ourselves.

When we let go of painful, troublesome thoughts of yesterday, we are letting go of negative energy, or as we say, baggage, which we are carrying around with us.

It does us no justice to carry forward negative energy from the past. Negative energy carried forward weighs us down. It is important and vital to our growth to heal old wounds and clear out negative energy. If you are feeling weighed down with pain from yesterday, decide if you are willing to heal old wounds and let go of unnecessary pain to make room for the *love* that you came here to share.

Remember to bless negativity each time it reveals itself, for the contrast of energy enlightens us to choose well.

As we recognize the old negative patterns, we can then dismiss them and turn toward our alternate path of love. Bless the path that lies behind us. For without this path and all its ups and downs, we would not be the person we are today. Without this knowledge, we do not know dark from Light. To know the darkness teaches us to seek the Light.

Begin each new day feeling good about the one before.

When we can see our past with love, it is then that we have totally let go of any negative energy that may have existed. It is then that the negative energy is no longer alive. It is no longer dormant. It is no longer part of our make-up, for we have *truly* let it go. When we look back at a previous relationship and feel a sense of pain and anger toward the person we had that relationship with, we are carrying forward baggage. When an individual feels negative toward any *past* experience, they have not *let go* of the energy that was created at that point in time. It still exists and is attached as baggage today.

As we look at those around us with love, we vibrate an essence of love, and therefore attract love. All people at a Soul level are pure love. It is our human experiences in this lifetime that have assisted in forming any negative make-up we may hold. We can learn to love everyone in our surroundings, including those from our past. They are here to experience growth just as we are.

When we can appreciate family and friends and the experiences we have shared, without holding on to judgment or anger, we truly begin to live. Life reflects a whole new meaning. When we appreciate and love yesterday, we can live in bliss today!

LIVING FOR TODAY

When we let go of lesser thoughts, learn to love yesterday and all those who have shared in our journey along the way, we are able to live more fully in our today. We are creating in the now—that is why *today* is so important.

Today's thoughts determine tomorrow's happiness.

When we are feeling good in the moment, we are recreating more of that good feeling energy into future moments. The more we make of today and enjoy today, the more we take with us into tomorrow.

Today is our most important day. This moment is our most important moment.

When we learn to live for today and deliberately create in each moment, our life becomes richer and fuller. We become more alive. We become the creator that we came here to be. When we learn to live this way, we feel a continual sense of freedom and upliftment.

As you go about each day, remind yourself that you are molding your tomorrow. See yourself as an artist with your paintbrush, or a sculptor with your clay, for that is exactly what you are, a creator, and this wonderful unique piece of art is your life. Whether we do it deliberately or unintentionally, we are indeed creating our piece of art today.

See yourself as the artist or sculptor that you desire to be, creating intentionally the art form of your life as you choose. One hundred percent of this art form is your responsibility. If you love your art form, or even if you dislike it, you are responsible for absolutely one hundred percent of the creativity in circumstances, events, or items that come your way. Every single piece was invited and molded through *your* focused attention.

When we apply deliberate focus and feel our passionate energy soar from within, we truly know that we are, in that moment, an artist applying our magnetizing power to invite and mold whatever it is that we are focusing upon.

When we truly believe in our creative ability, our faith of today opens up doors of tomorrow and intentional manifestations will start flooding into our life.

Your deliberate, passionate, focused energy, coupled with your true faith of today, will provide you with the most magnificent art life form of tomorrow!

YESTERDAY IS GONE, TODAY IS BLISSFUL, AND TOMORROW LOOKS GRAND

When we are living through our Higher Self, we are letting go of yesterday, living for today, and creating a grand tomorrow. In this state, we are connected to our Soul and hearing the messages our Soul is sending us. We are intentionally creating our life journey. It is here in this moment that we feel blissful. We feel the love inside and emanate it to others. We know we are creators, and we take responsibility for all our life events. We have achieved clarity.

When we feel this blissful, life takes on a whole new meaning. We realize life was meant to be this joyous with everlasting abundance. It was really supposed to be this good.

Living in the Here and Now

When we let go and relax, we are connected with our Soul and are easily led to our manifestations. When we have faith, we open the gateway to Universal Energy and allow everything to flow to us.

Our first step to living through our Higher Self and witnessing a blissful life full of wondrous manifestations is to learn to love yesterday, by working on our inner child to clear out negative energy that is standing in our way. Next, learn to let go and live for today. Enjoy today as much as we can, for the energy we emit today is determining our tomorrow. Finally, deliberately create and flaunt that fabulous artist style you know is buried within, and create the grandest tomorrow you can possibly dream. Look to tomorrow with fearless energy. Look to tomorrow with love. Know that tomorrow will unveil all of your wondrous creations.

Invite tomorrow with open arms. Know that your tomorrow will be delightful as you radiate from your power of now!

Tomorrow can be as grand as you wish it to be. Never underestimate your power to attract an abundance of love, an abundance of well-being, and an abundance of wealth. We are equal creators. We are each gifted the same power with which to create.

So, to live life through your Higher Self and to make life the ultimate journey through your highest choices, love yesterday, enjoy and appreciate your blissful today, intentionally create fearlessly along the way, and you are without a doubt creating the grandest tomorrow!

THE ART OF CREATION

The art of creation is to *directly* and *deliberately* focus our attention on the items, circumstances, and events that we wish to enter our lives.

As we direct our attention, we direct our paintbrush.

Paint your day tomorrow. How do you wish it to unfold? Keep in mind that major manifestations do not appear overnight, unless of course your energy is completely aligned. Ponder the little things that you can say or do that will make somebody's day and your day brighter. Take a few moments now and paint your day tomorrow in your mind.

As you follow your Inner Guidance tomorrow, you will be led about your painted day. However, you must listen to that Inner Guidance; it is there for good reason and will lead you to each desire. There may be some pre-created energy from days before that finds its place in your day. Let go of anything that does not align with the colors you have chosen. Then as you deliberately direct your paintbrush each day, the days ahead will begin to unfold to align with your art of desire.

Paint each moment as you would wish to live in the next!

Deliberate focus of attention can take time to develop. When I miscreate, I find it helpful to look back and uncover any thought patterns that may have assisted toward my creation. This helps me to take responsibility for what is happening in my life. It also helps me to understand the importance of maintaining deliberate focus.

It is important to gain our control back in deliberately creating our own vibrational energy tones that we are receiving and sending. In order to do this, we need to pay more attention to what thoughts we are processing and to what feelings are being felt.

Once you begin to understand your creative power, life starts to take on a whole new meaning. Doors begin to open, as new manifestations flow through. Possibly, these are manifestations that you have desired for a long time. Maybe you never received these manifestations because you never quite believed you could have them?

Happy thoughts produce positive emanating energy. Negative thoughts produce negative emanating energy. You have a choice. Remember, as you go about your thoughts that you *always* have a choice.

If for some reason you do not notice an immediate change in your daily unfolding of events, be patient with yourself. Give yourself time to get used to this new way of thinking. *Ask* to be a great creator. *Ask* to receive all that you desire. Your choice is always in this moment; choice for color, blending, and forming. Paint wisely, lovingly, and intentionally today!

Are you beginning to feel those golden keys—the keys that connect you to your Soul, to your ultimate happiness, and to your magnificent creative ability? Begin to use those golden keys. Begin to unlock the magic of your creative power. Then open the door wide to your full creative potential. As you become the creator that you naturally came here to be, you begin to realize you can be, do, and have *anything* that you truly desire.

Are you beginning to feel your power of worth?

*Sow and you shall reap

*Believe and it is yours

*Give and you will receive

*Love and you will be loved

We are indeed creators in our every right. We are all a part of the magnificent *God-Love-Energy* that exists everywhere. We are a part of the *All-That-Is*. And we are here to create beyond what is and to reap all that we desire!

Part 3

AWAKENING
TO THE HARMONY
WITHIN

***

A selfish act from the heart fills our
cup with love...

Chapter 8

Awakening to the Truth

SPIRITUAL AWAKENING

As mankind undergoes a fascinating Spiritual Awakening, we learn of our ability to create as human beings with the assistance of our Spiritual Selves. Through this process, we are developing a new awareness in regards to our past existence, current existence, and future existence. As this knowledge strengthens, our awakening increases; thus igniting a domino effect of masses growing toward the Light of Love.

Our society has grown together through good and bad, love and evil, bliss and pain. No individual is better or worse than any other. The only difference that each of us holds is the direction to the Light—or in other words, the direction to God-Love-Energy. That is what awakening means, being awakened to our *Path of Light,* where *God-Love-Energy* exists. We each have freedom of choice—to face the Light, or not.

By following the knowledge in this book, you are receiving the tools to assist you in finding your direction to the Light. In time, more and more will find their way to the Light—to pure happiness, true love, and a blissful journey. In the meantime, it is our loving task to uplift those around us and to defuse our anger, frustrations, anxiety, etc. When we learn to let go of lesser energies, we can live blissfully in our surroundings and love it for all that it is.

As we each awaken, we will turn toward the Light of Love. This process happens by taking our personal journey toward the upliftment of self-love, then emanating that self-love into a magical beam of unconditional love, thus creating a harmonizing energy to vibrate in and around our existence.

When we harmonize with our fellow people, we are harmonizing with the Light. As we move toward Love, we move toward the Light. As we move away from Love, we move away from the Light.

LOVING CONDITIONS UNCONDITIONALLY

We have a choice in each moment how we wish to be affected by our surroundings. It is through our attitudinal response that we are choosing. In most cases, we are unintentionally choosing. When we begin to intentionally choose, we learn to take responsibility for the choices we make in each step. It is then that we gain a brighter awareness of our ability to harmonize with all of our surroundings.

Remember the motto…choose and choose well from the *Smorgasbord of Life*. When you have made your choice, accept responsibility for that choice, making the most of that choice while it is present in your life. If conditions exist within that choice, then you accepted those conditions when you chose, so you have an agreement to those preset conditions. For example, a working environment can, at times, place conditions on the way that we dress, wear our hair, etc. We have chosen to accept this position with any preset conditions. It is a matter of accepting the rules that have been set in place. Nobody really likes to be caught up in too many conditions. However, when we can accept these preset conditions, realizing that we are in the driver's seat and the choice to stay is always our own, we begin to take responsibility and realize the *power is in the choosing.*

Let's take a look at an example:

Jayne accepted a role in pharmaceutical sales. She was advised prior to accepting the role that she was required to wear a uniform. Jayne wasn't happy about wearing a uniform. However, she needed to find employment, as bills were due and she had been unemployed for three months. So she made a decision to accept the position.

Jayne enjoyed the competitive sales schedule that was put in place. She also enjoyed her co-workers. However, she had a difficult time adjusting to the uniform that had been provided. Jayne just didn't feel comfortable wearing it and found it difficult to adhere to this condition that had been set. She thought about her situation. Her first choice was to find other employment. Her only other choice was to adhere to the condition and get used to it. Jayne really liked all the other aspects of her job, plus it was the best paying pharmaceutical sales position she had been offered. Jayne knew she had accepted this role with the preset condition of the uniform, and though it wasn't to her taste, it wasn't the end of the world to wear it for a while longer. Jayne made a decision to continue in her new position, be as positive about the uniform as she could, and look ahead to a possible promotion as the Director of Sales. Jayne had wanted to hold a position like this for many years, and after meeting recently with the current Director of Sales, she knew she could do the job. To top it off, she knew the position did not have the preset condition of a regulated uniform.

Jayne stayed positive in her position and soon became the number one sales person in ten states across the country. Twelve months later, she was promoted to Director of Sales! She has now been with the company for five years, and earns a salary she only ever dreamed about.

Today, Jayne is delighted she remained with this company and adhered to all preset conditions with a positive outlook. Look at where it got her. It was due to the fact that she did not allow herself to continue being upset about preset conditions. Instead, she worked at implementing a positive attitude, and then remained positive while placing her focus on a well-paid, future promotion.

If you find yourself in a similar position to Jayne's, make your choice. If you stay with your current situation, do your best to find the positive aspects. Take responsibility for what you have created, and know that you have free will in every choice that you make. In any given situation, there are always positive thoughts that can be found, no matter how deep you need to dig. Once you begin to focus on positive aspects, more positive aspects will appear. Take a look at the conditions and see how you can make them work better for you. You may be in a position like Jayne, heading for an amazing promotion, but you need to stick with the position and prove yourself first. Isn't it worth it then to let go of any conditions you don't like, accept them for what they are, and then refocus on the next position coming up? The more you focus on the positive result, the sooner that result will appear. If you focus on the conditions and allow them to bother you and stand in your way, the reward could possibly be delayed, or even denied.

We learn from Jayne's promotion that we can apply a positive approach to any condition by letting go of that condition, allowing it to be, and refocusing on an alternative aspect that we enjoy.

Each time we make a choice from our surroundings, it makes sense to accept any and all outer conditions that have come with that choice, while allowing all others' free will to create. If, at any point, you are stuck in a situation and it feels as though conditions are being dealt to you, take a deep breath and *ask* for guidance. Allow the way that you *feel* to lead you to a positive outcome.

Your Inner Guidance will give you the appropriate gut feeling to lead you toward the Light in any situation.

As we become aware of conditions that exist around us, we have the ability to accept these outer conditions without judgment and learn to allow others to create freely. When we release all judgment, we are allowing another to be, do, and have all that they desire, even if we would not choose it for ourselves.

The same applies to conditions in relationships. If your loved one is placing a condition on you, you can learn to maintain your appropriate desire and keep your boundaries in place. But also, love the condition by understanding your partner's desire and even though it is a condition, at the core, it is the way your partner has learned to express love. It sometimes doesn't feel like love at the moment when you are being asked to do something that doesn't match your ultimate desire. Though, no matter what, at the root of everything is love, even if it is someone reaching out for love through a negative approach. This doesn't mean we must accept a condition placed on ourselves in this way. When our boundaries are intact, we gift ourself free will of choice. We also have the personal choice to allow another to have their own choices, even though sometimes, we may not agree with their choice in that moment. Accepting that the condition exists and to allow it to just be, enables us the freedom to feel good in that moment. We can mind our own business and allow all to unfold around us, accepting all of our surroundings for whatever they may be. That is when we can live in this world unconditionally. When we can do this, we face the *Light* and others will see our happiness emanate. They in turn will notice our happiness and have the opportunity to *wish* for the same.

When we learn to maintain our boundaries while accepting and loving the conditions unconditionally, we are on an ultimate path to freedom and pure happiness.

Remember to take responsibility for all that you attract. If you continue to focus on conditions being set by others, they will keep boomeranging back to you. Let them go and refocus on what you *do* want to manifest.

We each hold the ability to love and let go of any conditions that exist in our surroundings.

BECOMING A LEADER—LIGHTING UP THE WAY

Some of us are leaders. Some of us are followers. The one who leads is generally the more passionate creator. They are the ones who believe in their decisions and move forward with little or no doubt. The follower is one who conforms and trusts that the leader knows best. There are many that are appreciative of another who is prepared to lead the way, as some find it daunting to make decisions and take uncalculated risks.

When we conform, we look to another and agree, creating through their ideas or projections rather than following our own ideas, our own values. It is absolutely okay to conform in this way, if the individual's needs are met and it stems from their own *true* choosing.

Those who are growing and awakening are choosing an open platform from which to create. They are utilizing their own power of thought and their own creativity. They are wishing to create for themselves, instead of conforming to create through another's existence. These individuals who stand out from the crowd are generally the ones who are self-employed, entrepreneurs, leaders, inventors, etc.

Have you ever had a dream to invent, become self-employed, or form a group and become their leader/teacher? If you are self-employed or are currently leading the way in an accomplished goal, do you hold a vision to expand and network to larger groups or organizations?

Pretend you woke up this morning with a whole new spurt of energy and excitement. Today is a new day. You feel the desire to step into new shoes and get more creative than ever. You have decided it is time to get focused on achieving that long desired goal. Take a pen and paper. Explain how you will make this dream happen. Pretend, make-believe, and have fun with this. Describe in detail how your dream will unfold and the people that will be involved. Pretend that money is no object; you have all the money that is required to get this dream off the ground. See this dream operating and working to your satisfaction. See it becoming a huge success.

Reflect on how good it *felt* to create and master a vision of success. Reflect on the *passion* that existed within as you achieved your results. If you truly enjoyed this vision, practice it again tomorrow, and the next day, and the next. By aligning your energy through visualizing, you will soon recognize the ease of being a leader, a decision-maker, and a risk-taker. In harmonizing and balancing your energy, you are aligning with Universal Energy, therefore *allowing* Universal Energy to deliver your desire, so you can reap any and all rewards. We are equal. Each individual holds the same opportunity for success as the next person. It is in *believing* in Self that forms the difference. You have the ability to Light Up the Way and make a difference in this fascinating world of possibilities. So give yourself a chance, take hold of those dreams, stand out in the crowd, and be *all* that you came here to be!

Chapter 9

Living in Harmony

CREATING HARMONY WITH SELF

Harmony is a positive energy we feel within when we are in a place of order and balance. Harmony can feel peaceful, or it might feel passionate, depending on the activity and mood. A harmonious energy never feels less than good. When all is well in our mind, harmony exists within and around us. We can cause harmony to exist when we simply let go of anything that doesn't feel good, and gently turn to face what does feel good.

In order to live a rich, full life, it is important to find a balance of harmony with Self. We naturally create harmony with Self when we are in a loving state with Self. Getting to that loving state with Self begins with owning respect for Self. When we own respect for Self, we only accept from our surroundings what is good and healthy and *adds* to who we are. We expect to be treated well by others. We also expect to be, do, and have all that we desire.

Self-respect is the gateway to self-love. And self-love is the gateway to the harmony that we all do crave!

Self-respect is being true to oneself and never stepping down from that truth. It is listening to and trusting our own Inner Guidance.

When we reach a place of harmony with Self, we feel light in each step. The weight of the world is lifted from us. We know all is truly well in the Universe. We feel that our connection is ignited with our Inner Self, thus creating a harmonious connection of Body and Soul. It is then that we are able to naturally reach out and attract harmony in others.

Creating harmony with Self first naturally attracts harmony in others.

CREATING HARMONY AROUND US

We have the ability to harmonize in any given situation. It is important to bring harmony to Self. When we can harmonize with Self, we have the ability to offer like harmony to others. We emit the energy that we are *feeling*. When we are able to harmonize with all, we become *one* with all and resonate together in a pure, loving energy.

In our Spiritually connected state, our basis of providing is love. In our human state, our basis of providing is love with conflicting conditioned thought patterns. So it would be fair to say that at the basis of every person's desire is love. When we have an understanding that all life is a basis of love, we then ask why does one person treat me well, while another treats me less? In our human existence, we have the ability to choose a loving energy or a fearful energy. All energy, whether distributed as energy of love or energy of fear, is initially formed from a deeper desire of love. Behind all responses, there is always a *loving* desire, but the response may not be a loving response.

In finding harmony with loved ones, it helps to view any negative responses they may offer as a form of love. This may sound difficult to do; however, when we break down the energy patterns behind the responses, we can always find at the core a desire for love.

Let's take a look at an example:

Lucy had been a largely built girl for much of her life, even when she was very young. She had been on several diets over the years, though not one had helped her lose the weight she wanted to lose. Lucy had an older sister, Faith, whom she was very close with. One day Lucy called Faith and was very upset. She couldn't believe that Faith had discussed her new diet with their friends at a recent barbecue. She explained to Faith that she didn't want the world to know she was on yet another diet, and if she did, she would get a loudspeaker and spread the news herself. Faith apologized and felt awful. She explained to Lucy that she didn't mean to be hurtful, and was truly happy her sister was going to try to lose weight and feel better about herself. Lucy accepted the apology and finished the call. Faith could feel that Lucy was still upset. She thought about it and realized that Lucy was upset because she wanted to *feel* better about herself. Knowing that other people were talking about her losing weight could not possibly help her to feel better. Faith understood that Lucy was truly coming from a place of love. Lucy was feeling upset because she wasn't feeling worthy when other people were discussing her weight condition. Wanting to feel worthy comes from a deeper place of wanting to feel love.

After realizing the love that Lucy was truly seeking, Faith decided to keep peace where Lucy's diet was concerned and mind her own business when talking with friends. She had come to realize that it wasn't helping her sister feel better at all. Faith called Lucy and told her she understood how she felt. She also told her sister she would support her in any way she could in reaching her desired goal. She then apologized for not previously minding her own business and promised she would in the future. Lucy was very appreciative of Faith's understanding; she expressed her love for her sister and went on to explain the new weight loss program she had just enrolled in.

To reach out harmoniously can be difficult at times where there is negative energy present. Look at the core of the issue. Then ask yourself, why is this person upset? What are they looking for? How can I understand them? You will find that at the core, there is always a *desire for love.* There is always a desire to be understood, to be heard, and to feel worthy. As we reach out, it doesn't mean we will always feel harmony returned from another. But we can still reach out with harmony. Sometimes, another is so caught up in their negative energy that they wish to stay right where they are and not feel any better. It doesn't mean you need to feel the same way. Look to their core energy and learn to understand their desire for love. Acknowledge an understanding, accept their position whether they are in harmony with you or not, and then let it go. Move away, giving them and yourself space, especially if you feel their energy is negatively affecting you. It does not help another if you continue to worry and fuss over them. Remember, time heals all. Offer loving thoughts, even if you are no longer in their presence, and work at rising above any negative energy as much as you can.

Let's take a look at another example:

Marie worked for a publishing company. There was one employee, Richard, whom most did not get along with. Others complained about Richard and seemed to find him annoying and pretty much a pain in the butt. Marie really couldn't understand why the others didn't like Richard. She kind of enjoyed his goofy ways and thought he brightened up the work environment. The other employees explained how Richard would get under their skin at times. Marie confronted Richard and asked him how he felt when the other employees appeared to be so bothered by him. Richard told Marie that he was not overly concerned of the others' attitude toward him. He also told Marie he acted up more than he normally would, to be extra annoying because of the negative energy he felt coming from them.

Each time we look at our surroundings, we have the power of choice on how we wish to view another's actions and words. We can choose to take a negative response, or we can choose to take a positive one. The power is in our choice in every moment. Marie chose to view Richard in a positive light, as she enjoyed his actions and words, and found him amusing. The other staff members chose to view Richard in a negative light, as they allowed themselves to become bothered and annoyed by his antics. If the other staff members had continued with their own work and *chosen* to ignore

Richard's playful antics in the office—offering no comments or criticism—they would have found his actions and words far less bothersome. What we give *focus* to grows. So giving focus to Richard's attempts to play office clown, whether it be negative or positive, was going to attract more of the same results.

It becomes enlightening to understand how much control we really do have over what we receive from others. We can see here why it is so important to let go of judgment. Judgment is not a positive energy, so will not attract positive results.

When we begin to take responsibility for what we are receiving from others, we begin to create with a more positive mindset. In learning to love and accept those in their differences enforces our ability to grow in love, thus creating harmony in all of our surroundings.

So what will it be? We can continue blaming others for giving us a bad day. Or, we can take responsibility and create a harmoniously wonderful day!

STATES OF HARMONY

There are two energy levels of our existence that bring us to a Natural State of Harmony with Self. One is a *state of peace* and the other is a *state of passion.*

Whether we are in a relaxed, peaceful state, or whether we are in a high, passionate state, we are *feeling* a positive energy within. This positive energy connects us with our Soul. When we are connected with our Soul, we are in harmony with our Soul. We are on the same wavelength and the same energy field. Our Soul is a make-up of harmonious, positive energy. The point of connection we make with our Soul, no matter how it comes about, is always a harmonious connection. It must be harmonious for us to connect. When we are harmonizing with our Soul, we are also harmonizing with All-That-Is. We then become *one* with All-That-Is.

Though each of these two harmonious states brings us into alignment with our Soul, each state affects us and provides for us in a different manner. Each state is equally important in providing balance and health to our overall existence.

We will now take a closer look at these two different types of harmonious energies.

PEACE IN HARMONY

When we are in a peaceful state, we are harmonizing with Self. Being in a peaceful state is a positive energy. However, even though it is positive, not too much creative energy is taking place at that time. This is not a hindrance. It is healthy to provide our bodies with a peaceful balance on a daily basis.

In our peaceful state, we are actually rejuvenating our energy. We are filling up our cup, so we have energy to flow, and energy to give. Giving time to Self is important in keeping that cup full so we have energy to offer others. When we hear someone say, "I am feeling spent," what this person is actually saying is that their *energy* has all been spent. Therefore, their cup is empty and they have no energy left to offer any other. This is always a vital time to take time out for Self and rejuvenate.

You be the judge of how much peaceful time you require to help you feel harmonized with Self. You will always know, simply by the way that you *feel* inside. It depends greatly on how you manage your energy throughout the day. If things get on top of you and you are feeling any form of continued stress, then letting go of that negative energy requires taking time out. Taking a stroll or relaxing in a park for ten minutes can assist in harmonizing your energies again.

After a long day, if there is an issue on your mind and you are having difficulty releasing the ill thoughts, a comical show on television can be useful to assist in refocusing thought and releasing tension build-up in the body. Laughing can do wonders for tense bodies and can assist us in reconnecting to our relaxed, free-flowing state.

Work at harmonizing your energies, so you feel balanced throughout the day. Take breaks when you require them and give to yourself. Be patient with yourself, especially in the beginning when you are learning to be in control of your own energies. Always be kind to yourself. The kinder you are with Self, the more peaceful you will *feel* within. Many people are unkind to Self as they take on large amounts of stress throughout the day. They don't pay attention to their body by taking breaks to assist in releasing negative energy. Instead, they run themselves into the ground, and then wonder why they are feeling ill so often and their bodies don't want to keep going. Many of us have grown to believe that running ourselves into the ground is something that we must endure. We give and give of our energy and don't replenish it. We walk around with a cup half-full much of the time. Take a moment and ask yourself—when you last felt *you* had a cup that was full and overflowing?

As time goes by, it will become easier to harmonize your energy and bring more peace into your life. Soon you will be a master and in complete control over how you *feel* in every way. The choice is yours to take time out, engage in a harmonious, peaceful energy, and refill that cup each and every day.

When we have given ourselves adequate, peaceful time, we begin to feel passionate to flow and move the energy that we have stored. We feel like giving. We now have much energy to give.

To balance Self, we move from a peaceful energy to a passionate energy, like the ebb and flow of the sea's tide. We fill the cup and then we give. We restore the energy and then we give again. We must always give to Self first, so we then have something to give away.

PASSION IN HARMONY

As we become passionate toward a desire, we are aligning our energy with that desire. As we align our energy, we reach harmony with that desire. We must harmonize first with a desire before we are able to receive it. The way that we harmonize with a desire is to get passionate, think about it, ponder it, and get passionate some more, until we basically *feel* that we can *have* the desire. When our energy is aligned with our desire, we are in sync with our desire. We are in harmony with it.

When we become passionate, we emit a pure, positive energy, connecting us to All-That-Is—and to our desire.

To get to a passionate place requires focus on absolutely anything in your world that makes you *feel* good. The more positive focus you place on that subject, the more passionate you will become. Passion is our reason for existence. Passion makes the world go around. It is why dreams are created. It gives us reason to reach to the stars. When we reach high levels of passionate energy, we find that ultimate, harmonious state with All-That-Is.

Build harmony with yourself and all around you. Find beauty in all that you see. Find passion in all that you do!

If you don't feel passionate about something today, *ask* to know what it is that will make your heart sing. You will soon *feel* the desire rise from within. And you will soon find yourself harmonizing with your new desire. There is always something around the corner to get passionate about. New desires are always being born.

MASTERING THE HARMONY

Try to notice your feelings throughout the day and endeavor to find your harmonious state, whether you witness a *state of peace* or a *state of passion*. Both states include positive energies and both bring us into alignment with our Soul.

When we do not feel harmonious and connected, we are then in a place of miscreating. When we are in a harmonious feeling place, we are on track and are heading toward all that we desire. It is like a never-ending circle of life. We get passionate and extend our energy. We then get peaceful and rejuvenate our energy. We then get passionate and extend our energy. We then get peaceful and rejuvenate our energy, and so on. Your body will always inform you of its need to rejuvenate. Your body will also always inform you when it is ready to extend its energy. When you pay attention to your Inner Guidance, you will always be *aware* of your body's requirements.

As Beings, we behold the ability to will peace. As Creators, we behold the power to emanate passion. As a part of All-That-Is, we behold the power to dream, manifest all that our heart desires, and move beyond our current stand. All is possible when we understand our capability.

When we can align ourselves to harmonize with All-That-Is, then All-That-Is will reveal to us all that we can truly BE!

When you can be *selfish* enough to get harmonious with yourself and turn within, you will have more love to emanate to this world than you ever knew existed. It's time to get connected! And it's time to get harmonious!

Ask to feel good and *ask* to feel harmony within. It is on its way. Harmony attracts more harmony. Things can only get better and better!

If you can FEEL it...then you know you can have it!

Chapter 10

It's All About Energy

ENERGY IS EVERYWHERE

Work at feeling the energy in and around your body. After all, it is all about energy. Throughout the day, at times, stop and ask yourself how your energy is feeling within you? Also ask yourself how the energy is feeling around you? Throughout this book, we are basically discussing *energy* and how Self emits and evokes *energy*.

All energy that we emit becomes a part of our make-up. It becomes a part of the person that we are.

Our thoughts and feelings together form energy. The energy lines up with harmonizing energies from our surroundings. It is then manifested into our physical existence as circumstances and matter that is seen and felt as is similar to our imaginative, original thoughts and feelings.

Once we cease to focus on a particular subject, that energy type in our make-up becomes stagnant but remains a part of our make-up. It will not attract unless we make that energy alive again with focus.

Energy fields are formed from our point of focus. And our energy fields are continually evolving and changing, thus determining our ever-evolving state of being. The more we get in tune with our energy fields, the more we will understand our need to harmonize our state of being. In our *natural,* harmonious state, our existence is a *pure, loving state*, which extends to and joins with All-that-is.

Pay attention to the energy you are emitting by noticing the way you *feel* throughout the day. Utilize your energy by applying positive focus, thus building your current harmonized, positive energy fields and creating more power within.

Energy utilized in a positive fashion is in fact like turning a dimmer switch up on a lamp to allow a higher voltage through, thus creating a brighter light. The more positive energy you emit, the more you harmonize and shine your Light.

Our willingness to harmonize our energy enables us to embrace the Light!

VIBRATIONAL ENERGY

Energy is vibrational. Energy is alive. All matter, whether living or non-living, holds vibrational energy.

Each one of us is energized with a series of vibrations. In our natural, pure state, as we enter this world, we are all vibrating and attracting on a pure, harmonious, loving note. As children, we are led and influenced by all those around us and take on many different types of vibrations. As we grow in our lives, we take on vibrations that make up who we become.

When we *desire* to feel good, we are in fact asking for harmonizing vibrational energy to exist in and around our body. A feeling good place is a harmonious place.

Lower vibrations that many of us have the opportunity to take on board get in our way when we do take them on board, disabling us from feeling totally harmonious and *free*. As we write or visualize to release ill feelings, we are minimizing and in time deleting those negative vibrations that are clouding our free, positive, natural state.

Every single person or object comes into our surroundings through our vibrational asking. Our *thoughts* and *feelings* form our vibrational asking. Then our vibrational asking magnetically draws to us *like* energies.

ALIGNING OUR VIBRATIONAL ENERGY

Our Soul continually provides us with knowledge and guidance to assist us in aligning our energy with our every desire. Our Soul knows our pre-desired path. As we focus on a desire, our Soul will then lead us every step of the way. When we are paying attention to and following the guidance from our Soul, we will create a harmonizing energy in and around our body. This harmonizing energy assists us in aligning our energy to match and attract the desires we hold.

In each step we take, our Soul knows whether or not the next step will offer an energy alignment.

When we focus on our desire, we can actually find a feeling place of where that desire is at in vibration to where we are at in our current standing vibration. At that point, we want to alter our vibration to match the *desired* vibration. Our vibrational energy that we are emanating, whether harmonious or not, is revealed in every moment by the way that we *feel*. When we are emanating harmonious vibrations in relation to the desire, we can then feel the desire is not so far away from manifesting.

The more we visualize our manifestation into our surroundings, the more we will feel our vibration align to match it. This might seem strange at first to try and match your vibrations with the vibrations of your manifestations, though manifestations can only appear when the vibrational frequency of the manifestation is aligned with our own.

Pretend you are going out tomorrow to buy a car—one that you can afford. Find the feeling place of that. Don't try hard. Simply relax into the feeling place of the type of car that you know you could absolutely go out and buy tomorrow.

Next—picture a top-of-the-line car that you would prefer to buy tomorrow, but know you could not possibly go out and buy tomorrow, and find the feeling place of that. Again, don't try too hard. Simply relax and find the feelings that would best fit that equation.

The first car is a vibrational match because you can already have it. That's why it feels good. The second car is not yet a vibrational match, because you *feel* inside you can't have it, so it doesn't *feel* so good.

The way to invite that second car into your life is to keep visualizing until it feels more like a vibrational match. See the car in your garage or parked by your home. What does it *feel* like to drive your new car? What does it *feel* like to touch your new car? What does it *feel* like to own your new car? Each time we visualize, we are altering our state of energy in relation to the desire. We are altering the way we *feel* about our desire. Your Soul assists you in aligning your energy to a place of *knowing* and *feeling* that you *can* have your desire. As you become more aware of energy aligning, you will feel a shift within as your energy aligns to match the thought of having the desire.

If you have difficulty saving money or feel a lack of dollars in the bank, it may not be so easy for you to find the faith in receiving your desire. If you are feeling a lack of money and wish to create more, then placing time aside to visualize each morning can assist in aligning your energy to vibrate a *feeling* of more money. What does it *feel* like to have the money in your bank account that you desire? What does it *feel* like to withdraw funds and pay your bills on time? What does it *feel* like to look at your bank statement when it arrives and to see your bank account with a healthy balance? If there is a vast difference between your current balance and the new balance of desire, it might feel uncomfortable when you first visualize. This is because the balance you desire is out of alignment with your current *feeling* place of *having* the money. For your desire to manifest, you must find an aligned vibration, which is a *feeling good* vibration.

The best way to align your energy is to take steps each time you visualize. Change the *feeling* of *having* the money one step at a time. If your bank account currently has a balance of $1,000—and you would like to increase it to a balance of $10,000—then (step one) begin visualizing $2,000 in your account. Wait until you have reached your goal before proceeding to step two. It may take a number of sittings, depending on your current energy coupled with your belief, to receive the desired balance. If your desire *feels* far away, I recommend reducing your goal to an amount that *feels* believable (in this case $1,500). *Faith* is a golden key in energy alignment. If you can believe it, you can have it! If you can't believe it, you can't have it! When you have increased your bank account to the desired balance, then move to step two, and increase the margin. How many steps or how many margins it takes to fulfill your goal is unimportant. What is important is *feeling* that you can achieve your goal, *feeling* the *faith* that this dream can be yours. Focusing on a believable result is the key each time to instilling one's faith.

A number of years ago, I decided to purchase a condominium within a new development structure near where I lived. The first down payment they required was $10,000. Handing over the amount of $10,000 involved drawing practically every penny from my savings account. If I were to go ahead and purchase this unit upon completion, in a little over twelve month's time, I would have to come up with an additional $41,000 (30 % down). I was nervous, not knowing if I could ever save this kind of money in that kind of time frame. The job I held at the time provided me with a salary of around $35,000 a year. However, I really wanted to purchase this unit. I had recently begun to learn and adapt into my life the power of my creative energy, and had already achieved certain goals from deliberately focusing my thoughts—though, not one had involved attracting a large amount of money, certainly not to this extent anyway.

When I began my visualization sittings, I visualized an increase in my bank account to $2,000. At the time, this amount felt believable to me. I saw it, felt it, and played with it. I used all of my senses to envision this money in the bank. When I reached that first goal, I moved on to step two in my visualization sitting and increased the margin. It took a number of sittings within each step before each goal manifested. I stayed focused on the big picture, the end result, not allowing myself to become worried about where the money would come from. Then something very interesting happened along the way. It had been around four to five months of daily visualizing, when I arrived at work one morning to find my job structure had changed, increasing my duties substantially. Fortunately, I was to be awarded for the additional duties. This created an increase in my salary to almost double my initial income! This was something I did not see coming at all. I was floored when it happened. Once the initial shock settled in, I sat back, smiled, and thought to myself—never underestimate the power of the Universe! I continued to visualize each morning and watched my bank account rise. By the time the $41,000 was due, my bank account had a healthy looking balance of $34,000. I was looking into avenues of finding the additional $7,000 when the developer announced that he had located a new lender. This lender was able to approve loans on this new development that required only 20 % deposit. Not only did this now mean I was required to pay only $24,000 at the close of escrow, but it also meant I could purchase that new car I had been visualizing!

Our Soul guides us in aligning vibrational energies to harmonize with our desires, and then leads us to our desires.

It's All About Energy

You do not need to worry about how, when, why, or where your desire will manifest. *Your work is to find the vibrational harmony with what you desire.* Universal Energy will line up the closest match to your asking. Through this process, your Soul will assist by guiding you through feelings to harmonize your energy, so you will align with the manifestation. When you are paying close attention to your feelings, you can *feel* how close you are to your desire along the way. When your energy is aligned, your Soul will then guide you through feelings to receive your manifestation.

It is the Universe's natural magnetizing power that lines up and delivers all harmonizing vibrations. Never underestimate the power of Universal Energy. Underestimating the power of Universal Energy minimizes faith. Remember, *faith* is a golden key every time you ask.

FEARFUL ENERGY

Part of our growth and creativity is in reaching for something more. Throughout life, as we reach for something more, we may feel some level of discomfort as we overcome fears that stand in our way. Fearful energy can cause us to be miscreative. However, it can also at times be beneficial. For as we recognize fear that is present, we can work to reach for something greater than we would have if fear hadn't revealed the unpleasant feelings. A ride at an amusement park is an example of when fear can be beneficial. We go on the ride and scare ourselves silly the first time. However, for many of us, once we have taken the ride a few times, we no longer feel fearful because we have overcome, or risen above, the fearful energy. To overcome fearful energy can be very fulfilling when it actually happens. For then we are floating on a cloud of *I am great...I can do anything.* That floating feeling is *self-love.*

It creates great opportunities for personal growth when we are willing to overcome fear. It is when we are not facing, or not willing to overcome, a fear type that *continually* resurfaces within our daily unfolding of events, such as guilt or worry, is when it can be detrimental. If we are hanging on to something, then we are not *letting go, letting God.* These fear-based energies that hang around on a daily basis can minimize or cut off our loving connection flow to God-Love-Energy, thus depleting our ability to receive. When we can let go of fearful energy, such as worry, anger, guilt, or complaining, we *allow* all our desires to flow to us.

When you are not feeling good within, you are not connecting *fully* to your Source Energy, meaning you are not connecting *fully* to All-That-Is. Worry seems to play a big role in our lives. We have become conditioned to worry about so many different things. Worry, I would say, is the number one reason for disconnecting from our Source Energy. Complaining, I would say, rates a pretty close second. Pay attention to what you are focusing on during the day and notice how many times you catch yourself worrying about something. Notice how many times you catch yourself complaining about something. Each time you catch yourself, tell yourself you are currently in disconnection mode, and not only that, tell yourself you are also in miscreating mode.

Enough fearful attention in any direction can cut off our loving, connected Source Energy flow. When you feel fearful energies surface from within, simply work at letting them go. Nothing is important enough to divert our attention away from receiving our manifestation. Fear can, with enough attention, cut off our life flow of energy, which in turn closes the door to our desires. Let's say goodbye to those unwanted fears that have been hanging around on a daily basis, and then say a big hello to all our desires that are lining up and just waiting to walk through our door!

RELEASING NEGATIVE ENERGY

Fear-based energies are a form of negative energy, and can minimize or cut off our loving connection to All-That-Is. It is not always so easy to forget about negative energy that exists, especially when that negative energy has existed in our vibration for many years. Negative energy becomes a part of our make-up—a part of who we are. Some of these energies lay dormant. Some are active. The energy that lies dormant today is not receiving focus. The energy that is active is receiving focus.

Here is an example of how Kylie's dormant energy was reactivated:

Kylie was turning thirty-two and her family planned a barbecue to celebrate her birthday. It had been a while since the family had been together. Kylie was very excited to see her sister, Catherine, and her brother, Michael. It had been six months since they had a family reunion. It was a beautiful, sunny day, and the lovely, large backyard held many fond memories. The jasmine was out in full bloom, smelling delightful. It reminded Kylie of when she was a little girl. Kylie was feeling wonderful. They gathered together around the barbecue and talked of old times. Michael said, "Hey Kylie, remember those silly glasses you wore back when you were in second grade?" Kylie suddenly felt an old feeling emerge. She had really disliked those glasses. They were her first pair and all the kids at school had made fun of them. Kylie began to feel upset and uncomfortable as she recalled the way she *felt* in second grade when she wore those glasses.

When the glasses were brought up, it reactivated the energy from Kylie's childhood memory, causing her to feel uncomfortable. Until we totally let dormant or active negative energy go, that energy stays a part of who we are today. In other words, we have brought that problem into our future, thus the expression of baggage, as we know it. When activated, that negative energy comes back to life offering an uncomfortable feeling.

Releasing negative energy requires rising above it. We need to go where the higher energy exists—the positive energy—and mingle with that instead. It takes determined, willed focus to rise above negative energy. When we realize that offering focus to negative energy really serves no purpose, we can then make a decision that we are "not going to go there and play that game." Giving focus to negative energy is kind of like inviting that energy to come and play. When we notice a negative feeling rise up inside, we can say, "No I am not going to play with that energy, I will find a nicer thought and play with that one instead."

Take charge of your life—don't let negativity take charge!

It's All About Energy

All energy that has become a part of our make-up can also leave our make-up at any time of our choosing. When we change our *attitude,* therefore our *feelings,* about that hurtful incident from our past, we automatically change the relative energy. As the thought changes to a fresh, positive thought, the feeling then changes to a fresh, positive feeling. This is when the energy shifts and takes new form, therefore altering our overall energy make-up.

It is our attitude that defines our energy make-up.

Let's take a closer look at Kylie's story regarding her first glasses. Kylie's attitude at her birthday barbecue was a memory of those nasty glasses that caused unfriendly comments. If Kylie would remember those glasses in a different light then she would shift her energy. Kylie did just that. She decided to recall what she did like about those glasses. She recalled the feeling of seeing the whole playground very clearly. She also recalled her dance lessons and how she danced well because she wore those glasses. She thought about the children that poked fun at her in school and realized that at that young age they didn't know any better. From what she could remember, almost every child at school had something about them that the other children would poke some fun at. She also realized that without these glasses she would have been lost. She was in fact very lucky to have owned them. As Kylie got older, her eyes corrected themselves and she ended up with very good vision. Her optometrist told her that this occurred because she wore glasses at a young age. Kylie came to the conclusion that those little glasses were indeed a blessing.

Four months later, Kylie went to her brother, Michael's birthday dinner. The dinner was held at their parent's place. At dinner, Michael again brought up the glasses that Kylie had worn. Kylie smiled and sweetly replied, "Those teeny glasses were actually a blessing in my life. Today I dance better because of them. Today I see well because of them. I love those little glasses." Kylie marched off to her mother's den to retrieve her little glasses from an old box where they had sat for many years. She brought them out and showed them to the others. Her sister, Catherine, said, "Oh, they are so cute!" Their brother, Michael, smiled and agreed. Kylie suddenly felt warm inside. What a great feeling to know that she had shifted that old energy and would no longer feel uncomfortable if this topic was brought up again.

Kylie's new attitude was formed when she made a deliberate decision to change her energy in relation to the glasses. Through the shifting of Kylie's energy, the other members of her family also saw the glasses in a new light.

Sometimes an ill feeling will continually resurface and try as we may to release it; it somehow just seems to hang on for dear life. If you find that an old uncomfortable energy is difficult to release, then as we discussed in Chapter Two under the sub-heading, "Shifting and Healing Energy," put pen to paper and/or visualize to work at dissolving the issue. As you write about what has been bothering you, then how you wish to now feel in relation to this subject, you can shift the energy in just a number of sittings.

Find what works best for you. Your Inner Guidance will *lead* you to your best results. Be in control of the way that you *feel*. You have the power to let go of any negative feelings. And you have the power within to *feel* good all the time.

When we don't pay attention to negative feelings, they can escalate to more powerful, negative feelings. Remember, like attracts like. Negative energy attracts more negative energy.

It is also important to remember that negative feelings are a form of guidance and indeed a wonderful tool, which enable us to realize in each moment when we are miscreating. Notice your feelings and when you feel negativity arise inside, learn to *let go* of those current thoughts. Appreciate your negative feelings that arise for guiding you in your time of need.

VULNERABLE ENERGY

Vulnerable energy is an *open* energy. When we are acting vulnerable, we are open to receive. We are inviting the unknown, while being aware that it may unfold as a positive or even painful outcome. Of course, we are hoping for a positive outcome; nonetheless, we are well aware that the outcome could prove to be negative. It is indeed a risky place to be in a vulnerable position. But to reach any and all desired manifestations, we must allow ourselves to be vulnerable. For without risk, there can be no reward. If we are not open, then how can we receive?

Many take a step back and do not allow themselves to be vulnerable. This may be due to previous mishaps that have caused some form of pain or suffering. In taking a risk, it is important that we take actions toward the desire and become accepting of whatever the outcome is going to be. We must be willing and able to accept a negative result if one should occur. Knowing that we can get up, dust ourselves off, and try again is vital in maintaining a healthy, focused energy. It is really okay to have a negative result. A negative result reveals to us what we *don't* want. When we learn what we *don't* want, we have an opportunity to gain clarity about what we *do* want. A good creator is always one who has much clarity. To gain clarity, sometimes we must fall—for example, like a child falling from his bike. The child is vulnerable as he climbs upon the bike. He knows that he may fall, but soon enough he will reach his desired result. The focus upon the desired result and not upon the fear of falling will have the child riding with ease in no time. If the child is afraid of falling more than he is of riding, he will fall until his desire to ride becomes greater than his fear of falling.

Children are generally more vulnerable than adults, as they have less fear and prior knowledge of pain than most adults. If we can take some time and watch the children in their vulnerable state, we can rediscover how to be vulnerable once again. Allowing ourselves to be vulnerable and take risks, like we did when we were children, will provide us with the ability to conquer so much more in life today. To do this, we need to continue to rise above any fear that is present and learn to trust and allow our desires to unfold. Fear is the only object that stands in our way—fear of the unknown and fear of the pain that may follow.

Allowing ourselves to be vulnerable and take risks provides us with the ability to conquer our dreams.

Children are vulnerable, innocent, and unaware of negativity that exists around them. When we see this, we say they are unconditional creatures. The child only becomes aware of negative energy when they are exposed to negative energy. When a child feels a continual emotional disturbance toward what is taking place within his surroundings, he may, with enough focus, take on board that energy type into his own energy field. Children are extremely vulnerable. Children are open and willing to receive. They are like sponges; they soak up and continually learn from their surroundings. Unfortunately, they do not know at a tender, young age the importance of reflecting negative energy. When a child sees his parents arguing and mistreating each other, he can't help but feel emotional discomfort due to the loving feelings he has for his parents. Children are always learning by viewing what is unfolding around them. As children notice and become familiar with negative conditions, they begin to protect themselves, meaning walls begin to exist. Then over time, they can become less vulnerable and less open to love.

Since children are unaware of negative, fear-based energy until they come into contact with it, we, as adults, are responsible to assist in providing a healthy environment for our children. The future is in our hands—to rise above the negative energy that exists and set a loving example for our vulnerable children, so they may learn and grow in unconditional love. It is our responsibility to assist them in remaining vulnerable and open to receive, so they may feel more at ease when taking added risks later in their adult life. And it is when we are paying attention to our Inner Guidance that we will be *led* to guide our children well.

As adults, we can be vulnerable toward positive energy while at the same time maintain a boundary toward negative energy. Remember, a boundary is something we place for ourselves to allow ourselves freedom of choice. All good can and does flow to us when we implement our boundaries. A boundary is saying no and not allowing oneself to become vulnerable to something that doesn't *feel* right. In teaching children, it is our responsibility to also set an example of self-respect. Children will then learn to respect Self and others, allowing them, as they become young adults to implement their own boundaries.

When we trust and listen to our Inner Guidance, we are made aware of any type of threat that may be coming our way. Our inner gut feelings will be strong in letting us know if danger is around the corner. When we ignore our Inner Guidance, we can walk blindly toward anything that may be standing in our way. When we are vulnerable in a loving sense and focused toward a loving outcome, we are inviting into our future all that is good. We can also be vulnerable in a fearful sense, focused toward a negative outcome, inviting into our future that which is not so good. When we are paying attention to our Inner Guidance, we know when we are being vulnerable to good or bad from the way that we feel within.

When we are in our pure, connected state and following our Inner Guidance, we are in a loving, vulnerable state, allowing all that is good to come forth. When we allow ourselves to be in this loving, vulnerable state, we are allowing ourselves to receive all good including any prior desired manifestations.

Vulnerability within a loving environment is a beautiful thing. It opens a door to all that is good. It blesses us with all that is loving. It ignites the beauty in all that we see. *Ask* to be vulnerable to all that is *good*. Vulnerability in this state allows us to rise above and leave behind all that is less than love. It allows us to see once again with the eyes we were born with...*the eyes of God.*

Chapter 11

An Art in Receiving

VISION OF OUR SOUL

Our Soul connects to us through a vortex of energy.
When our vortex is open, we are in receiving mode. Our
Soul is then able to easily feed Universal information to
us through this vortex. The more we awaken our senses,
the easier we connect and open this vortex, and then the
easier we will receive.

As we link to our Soul, which is linked to All-That-Is, we
have at our fingertips access to Universal information.
Feelings we receive throughout the day are intuitive
responses to previous thoughts or questions we had on
our mind. Intuitional responses offer insight to a greater
awareness, not always directly available when viewing
our surroundings.

Our Soul is truly our vision when we allow it to be. We
invite our Soul's vision by listening to and following its
guidance. As we allow our Soul to lead us, we infuse a
stronger connection with our Soul, which opens up other
doors to broader Universal information. The key is to
better connect with our Soul. When we are in a place of

pure connection, we can sense that a message is coming through. It is a slight awareness, but it is definitely there when we are.

Gut feelings are a form of *intuitional* guidance, which guide us on our path and provide answers to our questioning. However, sometimes a gut feeling can't immediately answer a question, for instance, "I wonder what the name of that song was that Chris and I used to sing together at Uncle Bobby's ranch when we were ten?" When we *ask* the question, our Soul gets to work on *answering* our question. If we are aware and attentive to our Soul's signals, we will be led to the answer. For example, later that afternoon we *feel* like listening to some music. As we search through the CD's to select one, we discover the song we sang at Uncle Bobby's ranch is a track on one of the CD's. Another example is, Louise trying to recall the date of her great aunt's birthday. She knew it was later this month, and she tried hard to remember it, but she couldn't. Later that day, Louise had a *feeling* to update her address book. Not long after she had started to update it, she found her great aunt's birthday written there right next to her address. Louise totally forgot she had written her birthday there, but her Soul didn't forget!

The answers are always there...we just need to be aware!

To be fully aware of your Soul's presence is life altering. It sounds quite different than how we have been taught to live. But when you strengthen your connection to your Soul, you will be amazed at just how much information your Soul passes along.

INTUITIONAL AWARENESS

We are all able to develop and strengthen our intuitional level of awareness. When we strengthen this ability, we can then *receive* answers more readily and with *more* clarity. Another way we can receive intuitive answers is to seek a professional reader. I personally, today, prefer to seek my own answers from *within*. However, I have found interest on occasions in the past to pose my questions to a professional reader. Many years ago, I did not believe too much in one's intuitive ability, though, over the years my view has changed based on personal experience. I have come to realize that when we ask, we can receive answers through various avenues. For the most part, we receive answers from within—our most trusted source—that is of course, when we are connected, aware, and looking within.

Other times, we may be interacting with a colleague, a friend, or a family member, for instance, who delivers an answer within the conversation without even knowing they are. To receive messages in this way can happen at any time, when we are *aware*. We will know if their answer is telling us what we need to hear by the way we *feel* within.

It is important to pay close attention to the way we *feel* when receiving an answer from any outer source. It is like feeling the answer within for the answer out there. It still comes back to the way we *feel within* every time. The feeling within will always let us know if what we are hearing is beneficial to our personal growth and desires.

On those occasions when we are lost, disconnected, and in pain; it can be helpful, and at times even life saving to receive answers via an outer source. If we have lost our way, others who are in that moment more connected are there to support us and help us get back on track. Even if we are not so connected, we can still *feel* if another is bringing us upward to a better place, or if they are bringing us down further.

To assist in receiving Universal information for Self on a regular basis, we must familiarize ourselves with our ongoing connected state with our Soul. When we become familiar with our ongoing state of connection, we naturally strengthen our *awareness* to receive. In strengthening our awareness so we may readily receive answers enables us to walk our path with clarity and purpose. Meditation, dreams, gut feelings, or hunches, for example, are the purest forms of receiving Universal information for Self. These you can trust completely, though it does take time and effort to begin to understand the art of receiving through Self. The answers come forth from within when we are listening, or aware. Intuitional awareness is being *aware,* so we are able to *receive.*

We are going to discuss next the art of receiving through meditation and dream states. These topics are fascinating, as they allow us to gain a better understanding of our overall connection with our Soul. However, to receive more fully, it is important to first work at strengthening our intuitional level of awareness. Placing quiet time aside for Self and also paying close attention to our inner feelings throughout the day will assist in strengthening our intuitional level of awareness.

A wonderful book I recommend that assists in strengthening our intuitional level of awareness is *Practical Intuition* by Laura Day. For information visit: www.practicalintuition.com

THE ART OF MEDITATION

Visualization and meditation are quite different.

Visualization is a technique used for attracting desires into our lives by applying deliberate focus of thought for a period of time. Meditation is a form of quieting the mind to assist in receiving information. It's a good idea to schedule separate times for your visualization and meditation.

The two techniques start off in a similar way. Both require quiet time set aside, a comfortable place to sit, and a connection between Body and Soul. Once we are connected, however, visualization becomes a form of *asking,* while meditation becomes a form of *receiving.* The receiving in meditation comes via a *feeling* or a *knowing.*

There are many reasons why meditation is beneficial. Quieting the mind is one, as it enables us to better connect to our all-important *feelings.*

During meditation, we receive a series of answers to previously asked questions. Prior to meditation, it is a good idea to deliberately ask questions, so while in the process of meditation, we can be aware of the answers that are coming through. If we begin to meditate without being *aware* of our questions, we can receive many answers in the form of stories, pictures, or words without really knowing what questions they relate to.

To gain a clearer understanding of how you are actually receiving answers during meditation, it is a good idea to choose one question before you start the initial meditation process. Choose something that is important to you. For example: When will I find new employment?

During meditation, you may also receive an answer to a question you asked earlier that day, or the previous day. As you ask, wonder, or ponder throughout the day, take notice of what you are asking or wondering about.

Now we are ready to begin our meditation. Fifteen to twenty minutes is a good amount of time to set aside. First, we need to quiet our minds. Follow the Meditation Technique in Chapter One, under the heading, "Let's Get Connected." As you endeavor to reach your pure, connected state, begin to release all thoughts. As thoughts enter your mind, continue to push them away and keep focusing on your breathing. You will know when you are in receiving mode. Each picture or word that enters your mind will not be a determined thought. Instead, it will simply appear in your mind without you putting it there. Back to our question: When will I find new employment? All of a sudden you see a lady walking down the street in business-like, winter clothes. You get the *feeling* it is quite cold outside as you watch her button up her jacket, as though she is trying to keep warm. Next, you see a mountain with snow on top. It *feels* like you are in the Rocky Mountains. You see crystal clear lakes at the foot of the mountains. You also see people hiking in the distance. It *feels* like you are focusing on the hikers.

You finish meditating and take a close look at these stories to see what they are revealing. You realize the hiking story could be an answer to a thought you had this morning—when you wondered if you would have more fun going to a National Park on your next vacation, or on a cruise. From the information you received, it appears the National Park with hiking would be a better vacation for you at this time.

The lady dressed in business-like, winter clothes could be revealing that new employment will come about in the following winter.

In understanding intuition, it is a requirement to truly open your mind. Answers cannot always be delivered in an easy-to-understand way. You have to be willing to spend a little time to research the information. Always take a look at the pictures or symbols you have received from every angle. See if they can be relative to any of your questions. Some of the time, you will find that you can quite easily relate to pictures or symbols. Other times, you will need to explore them a little further. As you continue to meditate and receive, you will find it does eventually become easier to decipher and understand intuitive information.

While meditating, it can be helpful to keep a pen and paper handy. Jot down pictures, symbols, or words as you receive them. Or, after meditating, you may find it easier to go back over what you saw and then jot it all down. Sometimes it is best to wait and write at the end of meditation, so as to not interfere with your relaxed state of mind. Though, as you meditate more and more, you will find it easy to jump back into quieted mind.

A work colleague, Sarah, asked when she would see an old friend whom she hadn't seen in a while. In her meditation, she saw an event replay from a few years previous when she had visited some friends during Christmas in Missouri. When Sarah pieced together the information she had received during meditation with the question she had asked, she realized the answer was Christmas time. A few months later, when Christmas arrived, the meeting did occur and Sarah ran into the old friend she had been asking about.

As we search and explore the information that has been provided, we are in fact strengthening our connection. When we strengthen our connection, we are enabling ourselves to receive information at a greater level. Our inner vision becomes clearer as we become more *aware,* which brings us into greater alignment with our connection of Body and Soul.

We all have the same ability to access our intuitive side. Much depends on how we utilize and strengthen our connection to enable us to receive information. As we place more time aside to meditate in this way, we will also become more aware of what we are receiving during our everyday activities. It is important to become *aware* of and *trust* what we are receiving in our every step.

Meditating can be a lot of fun and very rewarding. You will receive the information that you are entitled to receive—information that will not interfere with your growth. Answers will come in different ways and sometimes in parts. And you will discover more broadly another part of you that is extremely beneficial in creating this amazing life.

DREAMS

Many of us don't realize how important our dreams actually are. Our dreams are full of useful and vital information from our Soul. When we slumber, we are in a pure, positive state, enabling us to receive all information from our Soul. Dreams are designed to supply us with information to assist in making our path smoother.

During the day, our Soul attempts to feed required information through our vortex of connection. However, many of us are not always so connected, making it difficult for our Soul to send through the information. We are also not accustomed to understanding or even recognizing the use of our intuitive system. Because of this, we are not prone to listening to our Soul's directions. When we slumber, our Soul gets to work and resends the messages in an effort to supply answers to our asking. It also lets us know what we are creating during our waking state, or what we are miscreating.

Each time we receive a dream, we are receiving useful and vital information from our Soul!

When we heal our wounded inner child, or in other words, when we release the stored and ongoing negative emotions—also known as baggage—then our vortex naturally remains open much of the time, allowing vital information to flow to us. Not long after I had completed some inner child work on myself, and released some negative emotions I had been carrying, is when I started to receive intuition on a regular basis. It was then that I also became aware of intuition through my dream state. If you are having trouble receiving intuition through your waking state or your dream state, keep a journal handy. Then work at shifting and healing the energy, as discussed in Chapter Two, until you feel those old negative patterns leaving your presence.

For me, a whole new world opened up when I acknowledged that I was receiving through my dream state at night. I realized there truly is a Greater Energy that exists, and this Greater Energy is supporting me in realizing the greater power of my creative Self.

DREAM TYPES

There are two dream types. Each provides different sources of information. One dream type sheds light on our daily creativity, while the other offers light to previous questions similar to how we receive in meditation. To familiarize ourselves with these two different types of dreams, we will offer each one a name. The first we will name a Creative Dream. The second we will name an Intuitive Dream.

We will now explore these two dream types and their different messages.

CREATIVE DREAMS

A majority of the dreams that we receive are Creative Dreams. A Creative Dream is just as it sounds; a dream that reveals to us what we are actually creating through our daily thought process. The information comes in the form of *feelings.* These feelings are delivered as bad feelings, or good feelings. Bad feelings always reveal signs of miscreating. Good feelings always reveal signs of good creating. Creative Dreams are always delivered through the way that we *feel.* When you awaken from any dream, always ask yourself how you *felt* within that dream.

To differentiate between a good feeling dream and a bad feeling dream, we will offer each one a name. Bad feeling dreams, we will name *Creative Warning Dreams.* Good feeling dreams, we will name *Creative Uplifting Dreams.* Let's take a closer look at the messages within each of these types of Creative Dreams.

Creative Warning Dream

A Creative Warning Dream is an attempt to deliver an awareness of what we are miscreating through our daily thought process. This dream is delivered with feelings that don't feel good. When we recall a dream that doesn't *feel* good, we are being made aware that at some point during our previous waking state, we were miscreating. As we take a close look at the content being delivered in each dream, we can then determine our thoughts behind the miscreating.

For example:

When Melissa awoke, she instantly recalled a dream where she was driving to work. All of a sudden, Melissa slammed on the brakes. Her work files and handbag went flying as she screeched to a halt, narrowly missing the car that was stopped in front of her at the traffic light. As Melissa recalled her dream, she realized that she had been worried more than once about causing a car accident. Melissa realized that this dream was warning her that she was focusing on and therefore attracting a situation of being involved in a car accident. Melissa instantly made a decision to *let go* of the worrisome thoughts that were indeed miscreating. She also decided to practice some *faith* in her own driving abilities.

When someone says they are having a reoccurring dream, this means their Soul is repeatedly delivering the message through their dream state, as they are yet to realize the importance of that message. Some have reoccurring

An Art in Receiving

dreams that continue over a period of months or even longer.

A nightmare is a Creative Warning Dream we receive where we wake up sweaty, scared, and quite relieved to find that it was only a dream. A nightmare is revealing our miscreative thought process from our waking state. It feels like a nightmare, for the simple reason that our thoughts during the daytime can be just as frightening. Our Soul is attempting to get our attention during our dream state, because we have been ignoring the frightening, disconnected feelings we are receiving during our daytime focus. The nightmare definitely gets our attention. However, due to the fact that many of us do not understand the reason we are receiving a nightmare, we still unfortunately continue to miscreate. Until one day, ouch, we receive the miscreated manifestation, just like I did in the bank hold-up.

Do not be concerned when you receive a Creative Warning Dream. Instead, be pleased you are able to receive the warning, so that you may release those miscreative thoughts during your wakened state. Receiving a nightmare does not mean that this event will occur. As soon as we let go of all thought, we let go of the attracting energy. Work at following your Soul's guidance via your gut feelings daily. When you do, you will be led to what pleases you.

I want to reiterate that receiving a Creative Warning Dream is a good thing. Take note of the message you are receiving, and be happy that you have received this guidance prior to you putting too much focus of miscreation into a particular direction.

Creative Uplifting Dream

A Creative Uplifting Dream feels wonderful and reveals thoughts we offered that day, which are creating a positive outcome.

For example:

Vince had recently qualified to compete in the ski jumping event at the State Finals. Not long after he had qualified, he awoke one morning to recall a dream that felt absolutely wonderful. He was on a ski jump and was flying through the air at such a speed that his heart was racing. He knew in his heart he could win this competition as he flew through the air. As he landed, the crowd applauded and cheered. He looked up at the scoreboard to see he had achieved the winning score. He was so excited that he could hardly keep his composure. The microphone was passed to him while cameras rolled. Vince thanked his manager and his family for continued support, while the crowd cheered on. The feelings inside were overwhelming. He had never felt this good. When Vince awoke, he instantly recalled the whole dream. Understanding a Creative Uplifting Dream, Vince knew that this dream was an indication of the positive energy that he was placing toward winning the State Finals.

A Creative Uplifting Dream always highlights the fact that we are on track and are moving toward our desired goal. This type of dream always feels good. The more positive energy and the less fear we offer during the day, the more uplifting our dreams will be.

Thinking happy, uplifting thoughts will ensure we receive happy, uplifting dreams!

An Art in Receiving

INTUITIVE DREAMS

Intuitive Dreams deliver answers to a previous *asking.* As we go about our day and *ask,* our Soul always attempts to answer. When we are disconnected or just not paying attention, our Soul will attempt to redeliver the answer through our dream state.

We are receiving answers each night through our dream state whether we know it or not!

Many times throughout the day, we are asking even when we don't realize we are. We are asking when we say something like, "I wonder what that was all about?" or "I wonder why she said that to me?" or "Why did that have to happen to me?" Or even something as simple as, "I wonder where she bought that dress from?" Then you awaken the next morning to recall a dream of shopping at *Nordstrom's* for dresses. It can be as amazing as that. *Ask and you shall receive!*

Always remember what you have been asking or pondering in previous days. Then pay attention to what you are receiving in every moment. You may receive the answer during your wakened state if you are paying attention. If not, you are likely to receive the answer through your dream state. Answers are always being delivered, but for us to actually receive them, we must be *connected* and we must be *aware.*

You can have fun with this. Deliberately ask a question before going to sleep. You will need to match the answer up with a previous question, so it is a good idea to begin by asking only one question. As in meditation, if you have asked a number of questions, it then becomes difficult to match the right answer back to the right question.

I'll share with you an interesting Intuitive Dream I had some time ago. I was at the time in a relationship with a wonderful man named Ross. I truly loved this person. However, the relationship had become quite rocky and I was struggling with the decision to stay or leave. My father had passed away two years prior. Before going to sleep, I asked my father if he felt Ross was the right person for me. This was the first time I had asked my father a question since his passing. I wasn't sure what I would receive, but it did feel right to ask the question. The next morning, right before I awoke, I had just witnessed this amazing dream. My father took me into a grocery store. He took me to the dessert section where there were trays and trays of desserts. My father knew that like him, I had always had a sweet tooth. He took a tray down and offered me a dessert. He said, "Robyn, this is called the Ross dessert!" He then asked me if I would like to taste it. I took a bite. Oh my, it was so delicious. I remember thinking in my dream that I should share this dessert, even though deep down I knew that I didn't want to share it because it was so yummy. I offered my father a bite. He said, "Okay," and took a bite. Right away, he said, "Oh, I don't like it!"

As I recalled this dream I was blown away. My father had actually heard me and was offering the answer through my dream! He didn't like the Ross dessert. So there was my answer. I guess he didn't feel that Ross was the right person for me. Also, I believe the part about me not wanting to share the dessert was a message for me to set

Ross free, so he could move forward and be with the person that was right for him.

It can be very exciting to ask a loved one that has passed away a question as I did. Of course, we don't have to ask our question to anyone in particular, like a loved one that has passed away. All we need to do is ask the question— we *are* being heard each time we *ask.*

It is also possible to receive answers as you awaken. For when you are in that dazed state of awakening, you are still quite connected. As I drift in and out of sleep, I find that answers pass through my mind. This process is similar to meditation: we *ask* and then we quiet the mind. Try asking a question and allow yourself to drift. It is quite possible to receive the answer in that next moment. Answers can come in units, like a single word, or a single number. They can also come in a sentence or story form, depending upon how long you drift.

A good point to remember is that we will receive what we can handle at any given time, or, what is rightfully ours to receive. I don't receive an answer every time I ask, and sometimes I will get a partial answer. Though, I do receive quite a lot and on a regular basis.

We are all on a journey and we are all learning along the way. Answers are to uplift our journey and to get us where we are going, not to deplete it or jeopardize it in any way.

RECALLING DREAMS

Remembering dreams as we awaken can be difficult at times. In the past, I would remember dreams only once in a while. I began by *asking* to recall my dreams each time I would awaken. As weeks went by, I was recalling one or two dreams each night. Then as months went by, I was recalling as many as four dreams each night.

Keep your pen and paper handy next to your bed at night. As soon as you awaken and recall your dream, write it down; even if you only write down a piece to jog your memory later. If you don't do it right away, it could slip away. However, I do recommend writing down as much as you can; otherwise you may lose a significant part of your dream. As you begin to write, you will recall more of your dream. Sometimes I have one sentence to write. Then as I write, I recall more of that dream and usually other dreams as well. I sometimes can end up writing a whole page. Quiet focus on our writing actually keeps our vortex open and allows information to continue to flow.

When we first awake, a dream we have recorded may or may not make sense right away. However, later, when we are fully awake, we will usually find that it is easier to make sense of what we saw or heard. Sometimes as we awake, our dream may begin to slip away right as we are trying to recall it. We may see part of the dream and then see nothing. The more we *focus* on the fact that the dream is leaving our consciousness before we can grab it, the quicker it will leave. As we become anxious to grab the dream, the anxiety is cutting off our connection and the dream begins to disappear. If this happens when you try to recall a dream, the best thing to do is to *relax* and remember that anxiety disconnects. As you relax, you will stay connected.

Never be concerned if you had a dream in your mind and then lost it. As in reoccurring dreams, if that dream is something we need to know about, our Soul will redeliver it until we get it—sometimes in a different context than before.

Ask to remember your dreams.

Ask to catch your dreams before they slip away.

ANALYZING DREAMS

Analyzing your dreams can actually be a lot of fun. There are many messages being delivered continually through your dream state. To receive these messages, you must be able to recall your dreams, and then be able to analyze them.

Within your dreams, there are many objects or symbols that are used to clarify certain messages that are coming through. To understand these messages, you must know what these objects or symbols actually mean to you. There are many books available in regards to the topic of "dreams" that provide useful information to assist in recording what an object or symbol mean. However, the way you *feel* about an object or symbol is how it will be displayed or utilized through your dream—to assist you in better understanding the overall message being sent. For example, if a butterfly represents freedom to you, then when you see a butterfly in your dream, it is representing freedom. You may have never considered what a butterfly means to you, until you discover in a dream book it means "adventure." You then decide for yourself that a butterfly means "adventure." In your next dream, when you see a butterfly fluttering around in Paris, you would analyze the meaning to be "an adventure in Paris."

It really doesn't matter what meaning is given to an object or symbol. You might find that the dream book or the person next to you has an entirely different meaning than you do—that's okay. Your Soul takes note of all the feelings you have about every item. Your Soul will deliver the message through those impressions that you hold. On the other hand, how another person views that object or symbol in their mind is always the answer for them.

In taking a close look at Tyler's dream, we can analyze the messages coming through:

Tyler awoke one morning to recall an Intuitive Dream. In this dream he was traveling on a train with two friends. When Tyler arrived at his destination, his two friends stayed on the train. Tyler disembarked from the train and boarded an airplane. Tyler was very excited as he boarded the airplane. When the airplane took off, Tyler sensed that something new and wonderful was happening.

The summary:

First, what does a train mean to Tyler? Does Tyler generally enjoy train rides? Next, does he recall the friends and which ones were they? How does he relate to those friends? And last, what does an airplane mean to Tyler? How did he feel as he boarded the airplane and does he enjoy flying?

Any type of transportation is referring to a journey. The type of transportation usually defines the feelings that exist on this journey. As Tyler recalls his dream, he will recall the way he *felt* while on the train. He will recall the way that he *felt* while on the airplane. He will also recall his surroundings and other people that might have been involved, like his two friends. He will recall how he *felt* about the people present, conversations he might have had, and why they were on the same train.

Sometimes, instead of the actual person, we might see a superhero, a cartoon character, or a movie star. If you nickname a person at work "The Roadrunner" from the cartoon series because he is always on the run, then it is possible you may receive this person as "The Roadrunner" in your dream.

The dream result:

The two friends that were on the train with Tyler work at his advertising firm. Being on the same train revealed a journey of time, which they shared together in that same work environment. For Tyler, a train trip means a long and tiring journey. Recently, Tyler had been getting tired of his current job. When Tyler exited the train, he was leaving his current job. His co-workers stayed on board, as they continued working at the same firm.

Tyler exiting the train and boarding the airplane relates to a change in his environment. This change could be related to Tyler commencing new employment. Tyler's memories of flying have been happy and great experiences. The fact that Tyler has great experiences of flying, plus the excitement he felt as he boarded the airplane, is revealing that he will be much happier in his new position.

Since Tyler has become bored with his current job, he has been considering a new career that would be more enjoyable. This dream is revealing that Tyler will find a new career that he will very much enjoy.

As Tyler looks closer at this dream there may be more information. Conversations with the two co-workers might reveal useful information. Or numbers on the carriages, seats, or platform could provide for answers. For example, a number nine on the platform where Tyler disembarked could mean September is the month he changes employment. That is of course if Tyler had been asking this question.

OUR SOUL SPEAKS THROUGH OUR BODY

It is important to pay attention to our own body. Our Soul speaks through our body. When our body *feels* tired, our Soul is telling us to rest. When a limb *feels* sore, our Soul is telling us to relax it. When we *feel* like playing and engaging, our Soul is telling us we are energized and ready to give of ourselves. When we are *feeling* spent, our Soul is telling us to top up our energy levels, or in other words, take time out and refill our cup.

Our Soul understands and knows us better than anyone else and gives us guidance every time we need it. We *feel* the answers in a variety of ways, throughout various parts of our body. The more we pay attention to our feelings, the more profound they will become.

Sometimes, when we are feeling down about ourselves, it is not so easy to shift our energy to assist us in feeling better; especially if we are carrying an extra twenty pounds or more than we really would like to be carrying. But it certainly is doable. We do have the power within to change the way we *look* and *feel.*

When we pay attention to our focus, we can catch ourselves focusing on what *isn't* making us feel good. It is important to catch ourselves when we are *complaining* about being overweight, wearing large clothes, diets that don't work, or when we just don't feel so great. It is important to throw all those old complaints out the window. Complaining is a negative energy, it *doesn't* feel good and attracts to us only *more* of what we are complaining about.

We are being led all the time, even when we are eating. There is a gut feeling all of us receive during eating, actually a gut feeling that many tend to ignore. This feeling surfaces when we have been enjoying a meal and are beginning to feel full. Can you place this feeling? You might *feel* full, or you just might *feel* like you have had enough of the type of food you are eating. Does that feeling ring a bell? How often do you ignore that feeling? Are you surprised to hear that your Soul knows such things as the weight, size, and appearance that you wish to be? And is letting you know when to stop eating? Your Soul is also so fine-tuned with your desires that you may find that after receiving the feeling to stop what you have been eating, you still do have room for and feel like dessert and a coffee!

Your Soul knows all your desires, and all your likes and dislikes. Your Soul will tell you what you *feel* like eating, and your Soul will tell you when you have had enough. When you listen to your Soul's messages, you will *know* what foods *feel* best to eat. You will *know* when you have had enough of that particular food. As you see yourself the way you are wishing to be, you will be led each day to certain places and to the people who will assist in your desired look. You may all of a sudden get a desire to join a local tennis club, or you may wake up with a desire to jump on your bike and go for a ride. Always pay attention to the *feelings* that lead you. You can have faith in your Soul that the information you are receiving is one hundred percent, and if you follow all those *feelings* you will *feel* one hundred percent!

Learn to trust in your feelings from your Soul and be led all the way!

Visualize each day the way you wish to *look* and *feel*. See yourself getting on those scales and the reading you wish to see. *Feel* yourself wearing the size clothes you wish to wear. At each visualization sitting, ensure your faith is intact by taking steps, as needed, to assist in reaching your desired result. (Refer to Chapter Ten, under the sub-heading, "Aligning Our Vibrational Energy"). Visualize each day the way you wish to look and feel, then follow those feelings, don't give up, and remember—your Soul is with you all the way!

Part 4

PERMISSION
TO
SHINE

***

*I became selfishly aware…and
soulfully enriched…*

Chapter 12

Rediscovering the Love

REDISCOVERING OUR NATURAL STATE OF WELL-BEING

Our Natural State of Well-Being is that of *pure love.*
When we let go and relax, we release any negative
energy that may exist in that moment and naturally move
into our *pure state.* When we let go and relax, we become
connected and *whole.*

In our Spiritually connected state, we exist only as love.
Spirit is love. When man creates with love, he creates
through Spirit. When man creates with fear, he creates on
his own from a disconnected Self. Man does have the
ability to create with love through Spirit from a
connected place 24/7, when lesser energies are realized
and then released. It is time to understand, identify, and
release unwanted, lesser energies, and move into an
existence of continual connection with Self. Lesser
energies not only serve to miscreate, they also limit our
expansive mind power. Therefore, it is also time to move
beyond the limited mind and expand to a heightened
ability of extraordinary creativity. When you can fathom

the power of the mind to attract and line up with all *like* energy, then you know in your heart you can truly be, do, and have all that you can possibly imagine. We are powerful creators able to move mountains beyond our wildest dreams.

As we reconnect with our inner truth, we will be led to experience our God-given ability.

We connect to our Natural State of Well-Being again and again through recognizing the art of letting go. This provides freedom to be led and then to discover all that we have come here to be. Our sense of freedom can also be initiated by reconnecting to a past energy. By recalling a past feeling that once provided us with freedom, we can revisit that feeling place once again.

When we feel passionate, we feel free. When we feel appreciation, we feel free. When we are at peace and content within, we feel free. Take a moment and recall two separate occasions from your past where you felt alive and free. Then relive each one in your mind as though life was repeating itself in this moment.

This feeling of freedom can be found on a continual basis by taking notice of the way you *feel* in every step. Ask yourself throughout the day, "Am I feeling free?" If you are not feeling free within, you are in that moment not connecting fully to your Natural State of Well-Being. This doesn't mean you must be on a high all the time. Freedom can also be felt while you are relaxed and surrounding yourself with peace. Let go and relax into your Natural State of Well-Being and you will find freedom that is naturally yours.

Rediscovering the Love

When we are connecting to our Natural State of Well-Being, we feel free. When we are letting go, we feel free.

REDISCOVERING OUR FAITH

We are all born with faith. Unfortunately, however, many of us tend to lose sight of our faith along the way. It is time to rediscover the faith that is naturally ours and to rediscover our connection to All-That-Is.

When we have faith that we are not alone, have guidance on this journey, and can be, do, and have anything because we are *worthy,* is when we begin to live. It is then we begin to *feel* the *Light* and allow ourselves to truly shine.

Faith empowers our every movement. Faith provides us with the will to succeed every single time.

Recall a moment in your life when you felt a *knowing* in your heart that a desired request was without a doubt going to manifest. Recall the feelings as you engaged in the knowledge of the outcome. It may have been a dance class where you were awarded a medal for outstanding achievement. It may have been a volleyball tournament where you led your team through the finals to victory. It may have been a play at school that was a huge success. Or, it may have been an exam where you received top marks. Recall those feelings when you knew deep within that you were able to achieve your desired results. Recall those feelings that offered you *faith* with the *taste for success.*

Do you recall that inner sense of knowing where you just *knew* that all was truly well within the Universe? That message from within where you *felt* there was nothing to fear? Do you remember that sweet smell of success? Do you recall the small amount of faith it took?

It takes a small amount of faith to change your life!

With even a small amount of faith in our stride, we can conquer so much. It is a matter of letting go and reconnecting to our Inner Guidance that cheers us on— that Inner Guidance that we paid attention to so long ago. We are no different today. It is not a childlike empowerment that we outgrew. It is an empowerment that exists within us today and every day.

Over time, we have forgotten the value in being led. We have learned to pay attention to outside voices, and have allowed ourselves to be conditioned by these outside voices. It is time to release any and all outer forces that can deter us and hold us back from fulfilling our dreams, and then turn back within to where the real truth lies.

As often as possible, recall certain events where you smelled success prior to receiving your manifestation. Recall the inner faith you held as you connected to that sense of knowing. Reliving these events allows you to reignite that feeling place of certainty in Self, to reconnect to that sense of knowing, and to restore your inner faith.

Rediscover your faith within and move those mountains that you came here to move!

REDISCOVERING THOSE GOOD FEELINGS

As you turn within and rediscover your Natural State of Well-Being, coupled with that strong sense of knowing that supplies you with the ability to succeed, you will rediscover all those heightened feelings that come with it.

Feeling good means feeling connected to our Soul and All-That-Is. Throughout the day, ask yourself how you are feeling in that moment. Ask yourself, "Do I feel good right now? Am I feeling happy?" When you are feeling really good, don't allow anything or anyone to take that away from you. It is important to remember that you are creating your future in this very moment. A happy now is creating a happy tomorrow.

Others may influence your happy state if they are not feeling so good. In time, you will learn how to offer others upliftment in their sadness and maintain your happy state while doing so. It all takes practice and gets easier as you connect more and more to your Natural State of Well-Being, which delivers that sense of knowing, which leads us every time to *feeling good.*

It is a natural desire for us to want to see our loved ones happy, but in their times of feeling down, we must learn to uplift them to a higher energy rather than be brought down to a lower energy. Remember, focusing on problems offers more pain, while focusing on solutions offers upliftment.

Focusing on solutions offers upliftment, which assists in everyone feeling good!

When you maintain a high energy level throughout most of the day, you will begin to find a feeling within that you will no longer wish to be without. It is a feeling of inner happiness that uplifts you to a spiraling place of loving bliss. There will be little to no negative energy holding you back. You will continue to rise and be uplifted as you continue to turn the other cheek from all negative energies. When you reach this place, you will realize how much in the driver's seat you truly are when it comes to the way that you *feel*. Then you will realize just how special you are and the power of love that you hold within.

As you spiral further upward in a loving, connected state and see how much love and happiness you have to offer, then how much of the same comes back to you, you will know in your heart how special all mankind truly is. You will find yourself more loving and accepting of yourself and of others that surround you.

Our Soul holds the presence of our love. We can only offer love when we are connected. That's why it feels *so* good to be connected. Remember, you are your Soul. Your body is your vehicle for this lifetime.

Once you receive and get used to a continual connection with your Soul, you will quickly notice a discomfort each time you become disconnected. Remaining connected will become a whole lot easier as you come to understand the difference. And your feeling of connection will in time become so natural to you. So get to know your Soul today, that *inner you,* and work at developing a strong connection. Above all, enjoy your connection along the way and the guidance you are given—it is supposed to be a lot of fun, not a lot of work.

REDISCOVERING OUR SELF-WORTH

The first step toward creating self-love within is connecting to and learning to trust our Inner Guidance, for it is when we are connected that we are feeling good.

That is the first step, and it can bring us to a place of heavenly creating. Though, feeling good through our connection doesn't always mean we are feeling worthy. We can feel good about life and our creations and create with ease, but unfortunately, still not feel so worthy about Self. For example, a successful individual, through their connection and their faith, can create an amazing career, mansions, and multiple vehicles, yet still feel unfulfilled. Feeling worthy about Self is unfortunately the greatest loss we are suffering today. The truth is, we are creators and can create all that we can dream up in our mind. However, all of the outside desires we can imagine cannot assure us of a never-ending supply of ultimate inner happiness. This doesn't mean we should not desire and create. Of course we should, we are creators. What it does mean is that these creations *add* to who we are. They don't *make up* who we are! What we have been previously taught is that once again outside sources are the answer. We are still discovering that outside sources do not complete us. *Outside sources become the additional flow of what provide us with the potential in taking current thought toward new leading edge creations.* What truly makes up who we are and fulfills us to be whole is *love for Self* every single time.

When we are feeling complete and whole within Self, there is no room for voids. Inner voids exist when we are not feeling good about Self. When we are not feeling good about Self, we are not living through our highest potential. We may still endeavor to reach our state of connection and create well from time to time. However, living through our higher potential means enjoying our creations from a *complete* Self.

Nothing else can and ever will fill inner voids. To feel worthy about Self ignites love for Self. To feel love for Self is what completes us.

When we are feeling really good about Self and following our bliss, we are connecting with our truth...our self-love.

Have you noticed when you fall in love everything seems so right within the Universe? It might be falling in love with a mate. Or, it might be falling in love with a newborn baby. It feels so wonderful each time we fall in love. The reason why we name it *falling* is because we are feeling vulnerable, and when we feel vulnerable, we are feeling no resistance. When we are feeling no resistance, in that moment, we are feeling no fear. We know that it is okay to fall when we are not feeling fearful. When we *feel* a love for Self, in a sense we are falling in love with Self. We shed our outer layers. We make ourself vulnerable to our surroundings. We no longer feel fearful of relaying our true colors to the world; we stand proud and strong, we believe in our every move, our every word, and we let nothing hold us back. We feel *worthy.* We want to believe in ourselves this way again. We want to release all fear that stands in our way and see ourselves from our truth, our own sense of self-worth. We want to remember that we are divine creatures, each owning the same God-given ability to create with love.

Feeling worthy about Self is vital in reaching a fulfilling life. When we feel self-worth within, we do not need to seek happiness from *out there*, we just naturally own it. We can gain love from *out there* and that will assist in filling our cup, but when the love leaves so does the contents within our cup. To feel worthy within ourselves and know that we can be, without the need or requirement of something outside of ourselves, is a sign of self-love. Self-worth ignites self-love every single time. We are unable to feel love fully for Self when we cannot feel worthiness within Self.

Sometimes it is difficult from where you stand to realize all of your values. Choose a friend that knows you well and ask them to write down all of the qualities they see in you. Let them know you are reading a book and one of the exercises in this book is to have a close friend that knows you well write down your best attributes on one page. Any good friend would not mind completing this exercise and it would take only five minutes of their time. You may be surprised to find certain aspects that you had forgotten about, or aspects that you never even knew existed.

Self-worth starts with appreciating Self, which leads to believing in Self, which leads to adoring Self.

As we believe in Self, we believe in our own judgment of Self. Making it easier to release any outer judgment. Outer judgment is the thing that can place those bothersome vibes in our head, sometimes offering us self-doubt. Learn to believe in yourself and let go of outer judgment when it doesn't feel good. Outer judgment that doesn't feel good can influence our thoughts about Self, which not only affect our ability to feel whole, but also affect our ability to move forth and create fully. When we see ourselves through our own eyes of self-worth, our creative awareness is maximized and we emanate our ability to excel.

When we believe in Self, we trust our own awareness, and we believe in our own guidance. That is what young children portray, their faith in their own guidance system. Children with a strong sense of Self put their point forward in a very confident way. We wonder sometimes why young children have so much confidence and why they seem to know certain answers. They know at times, because at a young age they haven't learned yet to ignore their Inner Guidance. They still feel a strong sense of trust in themselves, which strengthens connection and ability to receive.

Over the years, many of us have been taught to distrust our Inner Guidance. In order to feel better, we have been taught to reach *out there,* claim what is ours, and by hanging on to it, it will fulfill our every need. I am not saying that creativity has negative affects, it really doesn't. Though, when we create from a Self that has inner voids and is not feeling whole, we are usually expecting that outside subject to assist in filling our cup. Our creative awareness is most important, but we can't forget the missing key, which is to *move forward and create in a connected state from a complete Self.*

A void is a hole when an individual is not whole.

Take a pen and paper. We are going to make two lists. The first list, we are simply going to *ask* for all the positive aspects we *know* that a whole, connected individual would truly own. Start by listing all the positive aspects you recall that we have discussed in this book. The positive aspects you *know* you are truly gifted with at a God-given level. For example, I wish to be a fabulous creator. I wish to feel divine. I want to know that I am worthy of all that I can possibly imagine. I want to feel alive with self-love. I want to continually feel connected. On the right hand side of your list, next to each item listed, you are going to bring each asking into the present tense. For example, I am a fabulous creator. I am divine energy. I am worthy of all that I can imagine. I am fulfilled with self-love. I am continually connected to my Inner Self. Whether we feel these listed items do relate to our individual Self or not in this moment doesn't matter. What really matters is the *focus* and *desire* we are applying as we write. In time, through our identifying and desire, we will begin to feel that we do indeed possess these qualities. Of course, we already do *own* these natural qualities; this exercise is assisting us to *remember* what we naturally already *are*. Once your list is complete, check in and revisit it often, adding any new desires, then converting them to present tense "I am" statements. As you convert each desire, take a few moments to truly *feel* the present tense feeling place of *being* that desire.

When we feel our natural completeness within Self, we feel vulnerable and open to give of our whole Self. We don't just offer to go part way, we are able and willing to go the whole way. It is as though our cup is now overflowing and what overflows extends naturally.

Those very young children who feel worthy emanate a sense of pride. They know all is truly well. They believe in their little hearts they can do anything. They are usually stubborn and don't wish to be taken by the hand. Instead, they like to walk on their own, for they know deep within their own sense of self-worth. That sense of pride and worthiness emanates self-love. It has not yet been disregarded at this young, tender age. It takes time to suppress the self-love we are born with. Depending on our surroundings and direct influence, it could take many years. If you ever want a taste of self-love, watch the toddlers and their strong belief they hold in themselves.

Recall those times in your younger years where you still had a strong belief in yourself and emanated poise and confidence. Choose an event from those early years that made you feel proud to be *you*. It may have been building your first sandcastle all on your own. Going to the movies for the first time with a friend, just the two of you. Receiving an award for the best finger painting. Going on stage to dance that very first time. Playing in that first basketball game. Take a moment to remember how it *felt* as you emanated poise and confidence, and the way you *felt* about *you* as you strutted your stuff.

Recall often these times in your childhood and relive that feeling of worthiness, where you weren't concerned what anyone else thought and your belief in yourself wasn't yet tainted. Reliving those moments will assist in rediscovering those feelings of self-worth. Remember, you already are worthy. Your Soul knows how worthy you truly are. You only need to let go of any lesser thoughts or any self-doubts that hold you back. Revisit your "I am" list often and turn those positive aspects into positive results!

Take responsibility for the person that you are becoming, and create the person you wish to become!

We really do own self-worth. It is our natural birthright. When we can let go of the conditional programming that has told us for many years that we are not so worthy, then we will naturally allow our self-worth to shine through. To fully appreciate and adore Self takes time of self-exploration. We can begin today to explore our self-worth...and unfold our forgotten treasures.

We naturally do own self-worth, we just need to let go of everything else and emanate what we already are!

REDISCOVERING SELF-LOVE

When we feel wonderful about Self, we align completely with the loving energy of our Soul. This is when our Soul pours through us, completing us with the purest love there is...self-love. It is our natural truth; it is our make-up at a Soul level. As we align, we now *know* the same as our Soul knows; we *know* our truth, our beauty, our worth, our power, and we resonate the same. The two aligning energies are each an energy of self-love—Body and Soul becoming one with the union of the same aligning *loving* energy. When we feel the presence of self-love, we feel our Soul, we feel fulfilled, and we feel whole.

What fulfills us to be whole is always love for Self.

Self-love naturally emanates Light. As you emanate self-love, others will desire what you have, thus igniting their asking for this gift that you hold. All we need to do to uplift another is allow ourselves to *shine*. When we shine from within, others notice. They desire to feel that good also. The Light is catching.

We each hold the ability to shine and bless others with our radiance of love!

Most of us, at one time or another, have come across an individual who radiated their shining Light; who stood out from the crowd due to their happiness and sense of inner peace. Take a moment now and recall at least two people who you have crossed paths with who radiated their shining Light. Remember how it felt to interact with each person. The way they held themselves. The way they spoke. The way they moved across the room. Recall their energy and their Light, and how you felt in their uplifting presence.

When you try to feel a loved one's energy, you will receive a reading as in a *feeling* of the love they are emanating. When you can grasp how they are feeling, you get a taste of the self-love they are emanating. When you can taste their energy, you can then ask with a deeper and clearer understanding for the same feeling place. The more time you spend in feeling the energy of another's self-love, the sooner you will attract that same energy.

As we come to recognize this wondrous place of owning self-love, it just gets better and better. Sure, there may be days when we don't feel so great, and that's okay. When we get back on track though, we will realize the difference in energy patterns between a lower energy and a higher energy. It won't be long before we become very clear which energy we wish to seek.

It does help to know that our Soul has always known self-love. We are yet to remember what we already know. When we let go, trust, and allow our Soul to shine through, our Soul will display what we already know. Our Soul will show us the way.

I recall a friend of mine, Adam, who was going through an incredible amount of pain in his life. I said to another friend, Veronica, "I want to help this person. I wish I could wave a wand over him." Veronica said to me,

"Robyn, just be who you are, for you are the wand!" I have never forgotten Veronica's words. Through her words of wisdom, Veronica was really saying, "Just be, shine like you know you can, and that is all the fairy dust you will ever need!"

I found Veronica's words touching, uplifting, and extremely helpful. In our shining, self-happy, and loving ways, we offer an energy that is like the wand. This energy can offer miracles of healing and assist in minimizing pain, loss, or suffering. Self-love is where it all begins. Just be as happy as you know you can be...*and then shine!*

Just BE happy and that is all the fairy dust you will ever need!

More and more people today are Soul searching. They are asking for love and happiness and are being led to people like you who are seeking the same. As a whole, we are moving toward the Light of Love. It is happening across the globe. Much change is occurring. With this change, things can only get better.

When we seek love in our life, love is what we will see. Those who have done wrong or have committed a crime may now be searching for the Light. When we are emanating Light, our paths may cross. We need not be afraid of people's pasts, for they would not cross our path today if they were not now seeking the same as us. When love and happiness is the dominant energy of that which we are seeking, we will find that others will not readily cross our path when they are seeking the opposite. As we connect more with Self, we will find that it gets easier to obtain a clear read on another's energy. We will know in our heart if this person is seeking upliftment or pain. We just need to trust our inner senses and we will be led all the way.

Self-love is an uplifting power of love that extends from within—it is beneficial to all those who cross our path, not just Self.

Chapter 13

Sharing the Love

COMING TOGETHER—ENERGIES ALIGNING

Relationships assist us in becoming conscious of the types of energies that exist in our energy field. At times, it is difficult to see or know what kinds of energies exist within ourselves until they are mirrored back to us. Relationships are perfect for this reason. They mirror back to us the energies that we like the least. They also mirror back to us the energies that we love the most.

The energies we like the least are energies that are non-productive. They hold us back from reaching certain goals and from witnessing that ongoing blissful, connected state with our Soul. The reason they exist within our energy field is because we put them there by focusing on them in the first place. What bothers us hangs around. What delights us hangs around.

Relationships assist to identify those energies that hold us back. They assist in bringing any issues that may exist to the surface, so we may identify them and release them, moving us one step closer to a more blissful state.

When we don't like what we see, it is a fabulous opportunity to take a look at the energy we are witnessing; and then look at ourselves and see how we attracted this energy from the other to begin with. Our energy always attracts to and aligns with similar energies.

We are all vibrating an energy make-up that stems from our attitudes and feelings about Self. We are also vibrating an energy make-up based on our focused attention as we view our surroundings. As we feel about Self and our surroundings, we will attract.

We have a choice in each new moment how we wish to view energies we have attracted into our surroundings. How we view them in the now will determine how they will reappear in our tomorrow.

To expect Self or any other to have zero issues or voids whatsoever is unrealistic. However, that's not to say that individuals are not seeking personal growth. Personal growth is the key. We are each learning and growing toward a more blissful existence. Some are growing at a greater pace than others. In coming together with a romantic partner; we will align with the partner who is currently in a similar place and with similar desires to our own in regards to his or her own personal growth and awareness.

We have a choice how we wish to view our partner. We are influential, for how we see our partner is what our focus can evoke from our partner. Of course, that is when the energy we are focusing on is available to evoke from his or her energy field. In many cases, how we see our partner today is built upon an awareness we have chosen during our past interactions. However, we again have a choice whether we focus on those energies or not.

During interactions with our partner, we choose how we wish to react each time. We also teach our partner to react with love when we set that example. What we choose to emanate is what we are *asking* to see before us, or receive from any other.

In a romantic relationship, when a partner sees our goodness, our Light, our depth, (for when we're in love we emanate these attributes) he or she will reveal our truth. This assists us to see our own self-worth, which leads us to understand that we truly are lovable. The only problem is for many of us, when that partner leaves so does the feeling or belief regarding our worthiness. It is easy to see our worthiness through the eyes of another, or through our partner's eyes. At least we had insight and were shown our truth, which is a blessing in itself. That insight might have left when our partner left, but the memory remains. That memory is what we can give to ourselves. We can recall it and remember our truth. We each are worthy and lovable Beings. We can feel that way about ourselves. We can feel that wonderful without having to hear it from another. We *can* tell it to ourselves.

Each and every one of us are worthy and loveable Beings!

How important is it to fill your own cup? How you *feel* about *you* is what you will give to your relationships. So the way to create wonderful relationships is to *feel* and *know* YOU are wonderful! So get cracking, fill up your own cup so you feel really, really good and then watch how your relationships unfold!

BUILDING HEALTHY PARTNER RELATIONSHIPS

In the beginning of a relationship we tend to focus on positive aspects in our partner. Focusing on these positive aspects in our partner encourages them to flourish in those areas of focus. What we give focus to grows. Though, as time goes by, certain flaws begin to surface. More often than not, when these flaws surface we also give them attention. As we give them attention, we tend to point them out to the other person. What we give attention to grows. As the flaws continue to grow, we usually give them more attention, leaving less time to give the positive aspects as much attention. As time goes by and the flaws are continually fed, different feelings begin to surface. He stops doing romantic things, like buying flowers. She stops doing little things, like making his lunch for tomorrow. The love starts to minimize and eventually, in some cases, doesn't exist at all any more. Then years later, we start to complain that our mate is no longer the person we married. We don't understand why they have changed so drastically, or why they are now revealing aspects like those other people in our past that we have complained about.

Relationships gradually weaken over the years due to focused negative energy we feed to the relationship.

It is important to accept flaws in the people around us. It is also equally important to accept our own flaws. While we are growing, which of course we always are, flaws are inevitable. Within growth, we learn love from fear. We learn from our mistakes.

Flaws are part of our growth. Know that others are learning and growing through their flaws, just like you are learning and growing through yours. When a flaw exists and we take steps to communicate our feelings to our partner, while releasing all judgment, we naturally create room to attract more of the positive aspects. Shifting our attention to positive aspects in our partner assists in forming more positive energy within ourselves. We then begin to move to a higher level of awareness, which allows us to see through unconditional eyes.

As we have discussed, no one is perfect. The person next to us is as perfect as we are in our own eyes. However, I want to point out the importance in understanding the difference between flaws and mistreatment.

A flaw is something that exists, that may or may not be negative, but nonetheless is something that bothers the partner. A flaw is never intentionally directed at hurting a partner. It may have existed as a flaw when you met your loved one, or it may have raised its head later in the relationship.

An example of some flaws would be:

- Not picking clothes up off the floor
- Complaining about the workday
- Forgetting to turn the lights off
- Complaining about the traffic
- Not putting the toothpaste cap on

We must realize that flaws can and will exist even in those who are generally positive, uplifting people. We can't expect another to always be perfect, for we are each learning and growing every day of our lives. In realizing this, we can learn to accept the flaws that do exist.

When a flaw exists, each partner could, with respect for the other partner's point of view, openly communicate and work at resolving the problem. After communicating, it is important to refocus on a positive outcome so as to not feed the problem. In many cases, when flaws are communicated, they can be diminished. In other cases, for example, complaining about the workday, it may be a matter of accepting the flaw and turning the other cheek so as to not feed the negative energy—knowing in time it will go away. This type of flaw is something that basically bothers the affected person in mention. It doesn't have to affect any other, unless they choose to allow it to.

Mistreatment, on the other hand, is not an act to take lightly. When boundaries are in place and self-love is present, mistreatment should not even be an issue. However, it is important to note here some examples of mistreatment, so we don't confuse mistreatment with general flaws that we can turn the other cheek from. Mistreatment is destructive. Any form of mistreatment requires action by the recipient through placement of their personal boundaries. We never want to minimize or ignore the negative side effects that any kind of mistreatment offers.

Some examples of mistreatment are:

- Verbal abuse
- Physical abuse
- Drug/Alcohol abuse
- Not willing to communicate and solve issues
- Belittling a partner in any shape or form

Mistreatment usually happens when someone is not willing or able to work at the relationship. Any form of mistreatment is unacceptable under any circumstance. Maintain boundaries and implement your self-respect at all times. Never allow anyone to mistreat you. When there is true commitment and honor, a partner will work through their downfalls to rectify their issues. In this instance, it is important to stand by your partner and support him or her through their personal growth process. However, if mistreatment continues to exist, the honor and respect is broken—and if the partner chooses to ignore his or her issues—then it can be an act of self-love to leave the relationship.

Be *selfish* enough to take care of your own self-love. If you stay and begin to lose a part of yourself, a part of your own self-love, things can only get worse. *When you lose your self-love, you lose everything!* When we allow ourselves to be continually mistreated, we are in fact mistreating ourselves in the process by accepting the mistreatment.

Always take care of your self-love first, every single time. Treat *yourself* how you wish to be treated. Filling up your own cup is forever important. Take care of *you,* by ensuring that you are loved and treated with honor and respect each and every day.

Treat yourself how you wish to be treated. Remember, you only have something to give away once you have given it to yourself.

Feeling *whole* means feeling complete within Self. Feeling complete within Self means feeling really good about Self, believing in Self, and owning self-love.

Feeling complete within Self doesn't necessarily mean that issues will not arise from time to time. Someone can feel good about Self and at times feel pain. Feeling good about Self means the individual acknowledges his or her self-worth, owns self-respect, and is able to implement boundaries when required. Issues can and will exist at times, bringing energies to the surface to be dealt with. When an individual is whole, he or she is not in *need* of an outer source to supply their overall happiness.

When we feel good about Self, we naturally see good in others around us. When we are not feeling whole, it is difficult to attract a healthy relationship. It is important to have a healthy relationship with ourself first, before we can expect to attract another who can bring healthy energy to the relationship. Two individuals that come together each feeling complete, for the most part, can conduct a healthy relationship. A healthy relationship, whether it is a friendship or a partnership, is built upon two people feeding it with healthy energy. This healthy energy is radiating from two people each *feeling* good about *Self.*

What we are getting from our relationships is what we are putting into them. It is that simple. When we remember that all of us are capable of releasing energy that includes either positive or negative components, then it is fair to say that we each have a choice in which energy we are going to focus on and evoke from the other person. When we focus on positive aspects, not only do we evoke more positive energy from that person, but we also feel really good in the moment as we emanate the positive energy.

Assist your partner by voicing your admiration in regards to qualities they possess. Appreciation for a quality you enjoy in your partner will feed that quality, causing it to continue to flourish in your presence. The more you assist your partner to shine, the more love you will receive from your partner. It is all about giving and receiving. If you don't throw the boomerang, then how can it come back to you?

In maintaining healthy relationships, the choice is always ours. In understanding our important role in the thoughts that we offer, we can be willing to take responsibility for what we are attracting from our partner.

If you are in a relationship today, take a few minutes and list five valid reasons why you chose your partner. Do these qualities shine as they did when you first met your partner? If not, then spend another five minutes here and visualize these qualities in your partner. Then visualize them for five minutes each day, for the next thirty days. Know that your partner still has these qualities within him or her. Know that your continued focused thought will evoke them once again. During your visualization, see these qualities blossom again in your partner, recalling the way that you felt once before when your partner did indeed reveal these qualities.

A few years ago, while attending an *Abraham-Hicks seminar, I heard something that struck me and to this day have never forgotten. We were discussing the impact that negative energy has on our partner relationships and Abraham said, "To be in your shoes and getting married, the wedding vows would be...till negativity do us part!" Then another voice in the room said, "Wow, perfectly spoken!"

*Abraham-Hicks Publications P.O. Box 690070 San Antonio TX 78269 www.abraham-hicks.com

I know it is not always easy to constantly focus on the positive aspects of our partner, though it is vital in maintaining a healthy relationship. It starts with making the choice to rise above any negative aspects or flaws that exist. As you take notice of your partner's reaction to your focused thoughts, you will begin to take responsibility for your part in the evoking. You will realize that feeding the negative aspects is only sabotaging your relationship. On the other hand, you will realize that feeding the positive aspects only uplifts and improves your relationship.

Negative focus sabotages and separates.

Positive focus uplifts and brings together.

GETTING FOCUSED ON THE POSITIVE ASPECTS IN ALL OF OUR RELATIONSHIPS

Focusing on positive aspects is important in all of our relationships. For so long, many of us have lived in judgment of one another. Unfortunately, for many adults today, our education did not provide a class to teach how sabotaging negative energy can be to our relationships, or how uplifting positive energy can be to them. The more we focus on negative aspects, the more discomfort we create within the relationship. If you truly want any relationship to have a healthy lasting influence in your life, then like the rest of nature, it requires feeding. What are you going to feed your relationship with? *Love.*

Take a pen and paper and list the three people closest to you. Then beside each person list five of his or her most gifted qualities. Once you have listed these qualities of your loved ones, take a few moments to really *feel* and enjoy their qualities. And remember, in all our perfections and imperfections, we are each as perfect as we SEE others to be.

As we remain focused on positive aspects, we are emanating a positive, free-flowing energy, which in turn evokes the same energy from others. The more we focus on positive aspects, the more uplifting our surroundings will become. Those who, for the most part, emanate lesser energies, will not be attracted so much into our surroundings, or will be attracted when they are in those moments of uplifting energy.

People close to us are very important as they mirror our attitude and like energies. When people mirror our likenesses, we then have the opportunity to learn and grow. Where would we be without family and friends in our life? How would we learn and grow if we were all on our own?

As we come to realize that we are all part of the same, it is easier to appreciate all who surround us. In understanding how our focus can influence another, we can then support them in their growth—seeing them as they are wishing to be seen, and seeing them as their higher potential. After all, we all came from the same place, and we are all heading to the same place...that of higher consciousness...that of pure love.

Chapter 14

The Glory of Awakening

TAKING IT TO THE NEXT LEVEL

It is important to understand the role we play as we emanate a healthy energy, not just for oneself, but also for our loved ones. To implement the change requires patience and understanding toward Self. Understanding and loving Self means releasing judgment and conditions we have placed on Self. Releasing judgment on Self is one of the most important steps we will take in regaining our true identity and adoration for Self. Judgments on Self are initiated when we believe we have done wrong. We then create a self-punishment in the form of guilt without realizing we are doing it. Self-punishment is the opposite of our truth—our self-love. Meaning, this type of energy could be the darkest and farthest away from where we are heading. If we are to find our truth, we must change our direction.

If we can take one step back from society and the trends of disbelief about Self, we will begin to see the top of the mountain and take strides to the next level of awareness. There is so much more than what many have witnessed.

The Glory of Awakening

There is so much pure love that exists everywhere. Taking our love for Self to the next level means shedding old negative patterns of belief which have stood in our way for a long time. These patterns stem from an ego Self—an ego Self that is attached to fear.

When we release the ego, we are allowing the old skin that serves no purpose to lose resistance and fall away. It means removing the surface layers that are suffocating our greater truth. When we offer focus to ego that exists, we lose our way and invite more ego energy. When we offer focus to love that exists, we find our way and invite more loving energy.

Many of us are giving the ego encouragement every day without even realizing we are doing it. It is time to rise above the fear and offer focus and encouragement to the loving energy that exists around us. It is time to feed the love and release the fear and take our love to the next level. If we don't open our eyes, we will continue to lose sight of our birthright. Our birthright is unconditional love.

When we come to realize our creative power and take responsibility for who we are becoming, a whole new world of possibilities opens. We create pain or laughter in each step. First we must make the choice. When we recognize the difference between truth and ego, we can make better choices. If pain exists, ask yourself why. Look at what brought about the pain. Then seek to diffuse the pain. Changing the attitude, which shifts the energy in relation to the subject at hand, will bring about a new response the next time the same subject arises.

Take note throughout the day of how you are feeling, and then take responsibility for the way you are feeling. Know that your previous thoughts have brought about this current manifestation. Take responsibility for what you are receiving in the moment, for it is a boomerang effect of energy coming about from previous energy you sent out; whether the energy was offered in words, or in thoughts alone. When you can understand this and learn to take a look at why you are attracting certain energies, you are well on your way to shifting and raising your energy to a whole new level of awareness.

All that each one of us encounters reflects Self. Co-creating with others assists to better understand Self, to correct our shortcomings, and gain clarity in relation to our true desires.

The first step in taking ourselves to the next level of awareness is to take responsibility for what we are attracting. The next step is learning to *allow* Self to be, do, and have all that we desire to create in our own lives, while always taking care of and nurturing Self in the process. The last step is to learn to *allow* others to be, do, and have all that they are creating in their own lives, while offering them love and upliftment along the way. In implementing these steps, we must choose to turn the other cheek from the ego, and choose to face the loving energy that surrounds us.

RELEASING EGO ALLOWS PURE LOVE

Ego is the fear-based energy make-up of which we have choice. When ego is not our choice, we have then chosen to vibrate in our Natural State of Pure Love. Many of us have chosen ego over love on almost a daily basis, throughout our entire lifetime. We have allowed our fears to get the better of our attention, and we have allowed these fears to determine who we become. If we continue to live this way, inviting the ego to take control, we will then continue to live out of fear. Ego teaches us control; it teaches us anger, denial, and pain. Ego teaches us anything less than love.

Ego and love cannot co-exist. They are two different energies. Where love exists by choice, ego has no space. Where ego exists by choice, love has no space. Unfortunately, we have come to believe that the ego is our truth, our will to survive. Ego is anything but the truth. The only truth that exists is love. In our pure, connected state, we naturally vibrate *love.*

A friend once quoted to me a translation of "ego" offered to him by a Minister from his local church:

EGO: *Edging God out*

God-Love-Energy exists everywhere and through everything. God created us in his image, that of pure love. We are each born as pure, loving energy. All that is real is what God created. Our Souls are real. We believe that the ego is real, yet the ego is not. Anything that is not love is not real.

When we are disconnected, it becomes the ego's choice; and to choose is a heavy burden on the ego, because the ego has only one choice and that is fear. So what does the ego do? The ego conforms.

Each moment we have choice. We choose to connect to our Natural State of God-Love-Energy, or we choose to disconnect from our Natural State of God-Love-Energy.

We have free will to choose in every moment. We have complete control. However, at times, many of us choose through the eyes of another. We see what they see. For how can we choose for ourselves when we are told that we are unworthy to choose?

As the ego connects to lesser energies, it tells us through a fearful energy that we are not enough to supply the answer. The Soul has the answer; however, due to the presence of fear, it has been discarded by unworthiness. When we are in our ego state of awareness, or in other words, our disconnected state, we are feeling fearful, so we latch on to another's thoughts and opinions, because at that point in time we are distrusting our own. When we are conforming, we are trusting in an outer source more than we are trusting in ourselves.

As we have discussed, Universal knowledge is available to us 24/7 and is always at our fingertips. So why don't we trust these feelings from within? Why don't we validate our own feelings? It is time to believe in *Self* once again and validate our Inner Guidance. It is time to step out of the crowd, to Light Up our existence, and to reveal our worthiness to the world. To do this, we must learn to understand and then release this ego-based energy.

As we see the ego in others, we are seeing it in ourselves. The answer in turning to love is to release the ego. This means that in our awareness, the ego no longer exists. We give it no life. Every time another acts from their ego and we feel hurt while focusing on their action, thus causing our ego to have a reaction, we have just fed the ego and the cycle continues. The feeding of the ego allows for miscreation. To cut off the cycle of the ego, we need to basically starve the ego. What starves can't live. The brutal truth is that we are either starving the ego, or we are starving the love. As we starve love, we starve our Natural State of Being, thus giving life to illnesses. Where love is being fed, illnesses cannot flourish.

In our awakening, we return to our Natural State of Pure Love, releasing all lesser energies. This process is named the *atonement*. Through the atonement, Jesus offers to assist us in finding our way home. What this means is that if we ask him to take our hand and lead us, he will assist us in releasing the ego, so we can relax back into our Natural State of Pure Love. We have freedom of choice in every step. To release the ego and find our way home to our Natural State of Pure Love, we must first *desire* and then *ask*. We must be ready and willing to hold out our hand, and then be led.

ALLOWING PURE LOVE—SETTING AN EXAMPLE

When love is our choice, then love is all we will see. When the ego bears no significance, it bears no life. All love is pure and simple. The ego is messy and complicated. It is time to rid ourselves of the messy energy that clogs up the pores of our existence and allows us to miscreate. It is time to *atone* and *release*. It is time to cleanse. As we cleanse, we make room for love. As we grow in love, we fill our cup—as our cup overflows, it flows to the world. Our love that flows to the world is unconditional. It is time to get focused on Self and get *selfish* enough to cleanse our energy, so others will see what we have and ask for the same. When others ask for the same, we then assist in cleansing the world.

On our path to atone, we are required to *let go and let God*. Let go and allow the shifting to take place for the removal of old lesser energies. Be rid of them once and for all, so we may reside again in that abundance of health we were all born with.

Simply *ask* and the atonement will commence. Your Soul, through its connection to All-That-Is, will paint the path to atone. The atonement is merely a shifting and releasing of lesser energies. It is the return to our Natural State of God-Love-Energy. In time, you will feel a different outlook, a different attitude, as you no longer reach for those lesser energies; for they have been removed and no longer vibrate within your being. It won't happen overnight and there will be work to accomplish as you are led to actions that will assist in releasing the energies. For example, reading a book, taking a class, or learning through a relationship that mirrors those lesser, undesirable energies. However, when it does happen, when those energies begin to shift, it will be well worth the effort.

The atonement is merely a shifting and releasing of lesser energies. It is a return to our Natural State of God-Love-Energy.

Your work required here is to let go and allow the shift to occur, while being led joyously to any actions that may be required. Once the energy has shifted, you will feel a difference. You will feel lighter in each step, for the dense, lesser energy has been removed and is no longer a burden. As you move toward the Light, you will feel and emanate your purest love. Ego will be no barrier. You will no longer desire lesser energy and offer no focus. You simply turn the other cheek. At this point, remember to pay attention to your focus, also to your feelings from your Soul, so as to disallow reintroduction of old energies.

If you notice old, lesser energies reintroducing themselves, simply turn the other cheek and offer no focus. You have the power to accept and include energy. You also have the power to diffuse and release energy. As you diffuse and release unwanted energy, there is no need to be concerned about owning it again. Once the old energies have been released, you will notice a difference that you will want to maintain. You will feel lighter in each step. You will realize those old lesser energies you carried around for years were a burden and not a bonus. At that point, it will be easier to turn the other cheek. You will have come to know that by focusing on the lesser energy, you are actually inviting it. Turning the other cheek will get easier to do as time goes by. It will actually become natural to you. You won't need to think too much about it—you will just naturally turn the other way while offering no judgment.

Take notice of the way you are feeling today. Make it a point to focus on positive aspects wherever you are. Positive focus attracts positive energy. You are always in the driver's seat when it comes to what energy types you are attracting. Positive energy is a loving energy. That is our point of connection—positive energy. Positive energy exists everywhere and through everything. It is the make-up of God-Love-Energy, which exists everywhere and through everything. We can tap into it at any moment in time when that is our desire.

Positive focus will always boomerang positive results!

ATTRACTING PERFECT HARMONY

We *are* able to attract perfect harmony into our lives. When we reach perfect harmony within ourselves, we will attract perfect harmony from our surroundings. To find this perfect harmony within ourselves starts with loving Self. When we are feeling love for Self, we are seeing the good in ourselves, we are nurturing ourselves, and we are able to forgive ourselves. When we feel love for Self, we know how precious Self is. We understand the importance of connection with our Soul. We understand that feeling good in the moment is all that ever truly matters to living a peaceful existence. We also know that when a painful experience does emerge, we can face it, deal with it, and return to our Natural State of Pure Love before it greatly affects our overall energy.

When we are feeling love for Self, we simply know and feel how precious Self is!

When we can truly accept ourselves for who we are and release all self-judgment, we will reside in harmony. Self-judgment is the form of fear-based guilt that holds so many of us back from experiencing a spiraling existence. Self-judgment releases an energy that lines up with and attracts outer judgement. The type of judgmental energy that Self receives is boomeranging back from the judgmental energy emanated from Self; whether that judgmental energy was actually about Self or about another individual. How we *feel* about Self forms our opinions about Self, which attracts similar feelings from another. How we *feel* about another individual forms energy that becomes part of our own energy field, and therefore attracts similar energy.

When another points the finger at you next time, ask
yourself how *you* initiated that energy to come forth.
How were *you* feeling that brought about that finger
pointing? Were *you* being hard on yourself in regard to
the topic at hand? Were *you* feeling guilty? Or, were *you*
pointing the finger at someone else regarding a similar
topic? Ask yourself how *you* were feeling in relation to
that topic.

When we know the power of our thoughts and feelings,
and understand each person's responsibility within the
realm of creativity, we can learn to accept all that exists
in our surroundings for what it is with no judgment. Or,
in other words, when we can truly allow Self and any
other to be, do, and have all that each are desiring; we are
understanding that each of us is responsible for what we
are attracting, and we can let go and accept our creations
in each moment. It is then that we will live in perfect
harmony.

*When we are completely accepting and allowing of Self
and others in the moment, we are living in perfect
harmony.*

Harmony attracts harmony. Disharmony attracts
disharmony. It is that simple. Understanding our power of
thought and feeling creates guidance for simplifying the
art of letting go. Harmony is letting go. Disharmony is
resistance.

It is in letting go where perfect harmony exists. It is in
letting go where we connect to the God-Love-Energy that
exists, allowing all that we desire to come forth.

ATTRACTING WONDERFUL ENERGY

The way we feel about Self extends an energy that attracts like energy. Every feeling that we offer attracts an outcome. When we feel good, we have the ability to attract good energy from others. When we feel bad, we have the ability to attract bad energy from others. In every thought we hold, we receive a feeling. For every feeling we receive, we emit a vibrational energy that defines the feeling place that exists. This energy that is released is the energy that enables each of us to intuitively read one another. This energy that is released also holds magnetic power that attracts like energy.

Each thought is powerful, just as each feeling is powerful. Every focused thought brings about a feeling, which either connects us to our Soul, or disconnects us. Each time we connect or disconnect, we feel a certain way. Connection feels good and creates a harmony within. Disconnection feels bad and creates a disharmony within.

Every time we feel a certain way, we emanate an energy that is formed from the way that we are *feeling*. Each feeling we offer becomes part of our energy make-up. The way that we *feel* in each moment is offering energy that is attracting like energies.

The way we feel about Self and our surroundings provides an attraction formula for what we are receiving.

It is important to understand how energy forms and how it moves between individuals. When we can understand how energy shifts and takes form, we can understand how to implement harmony into our lives every minute of every day. If it is our desire to have good feelings in the presence of others, we will be led to the right place when a pleasant situation will form with another individual. It is when we are paying attention to our Inner Guidance that we will be led to the right people at the right time to share good energy. We can trust the way we *feel* in regards to which day and time is best to spend with each individual. If positive interactions are what we desire, our feelings will lead us toward positive interactions. When we focus on harmony or desire to feel harmony, then harmonious situations are what we will be led toward.

Each individual's energy we come into contact with will, when we allow it, leave an impact after each meeting. A positive meeting can have a positive impact. Whereas a negative situation can, if we allow it, have a negative impact. I am not saying that we must have only positive individuals in our life. Nobody is perfect. If we are in front of an individual who is emanating a negative energy, it is our choice whether or not we take on that same energy. If we trust the way we *feel,* we will know which energies are negative, or which energies are positive. We will also know by the way that we *feel* when we are reflecting negative energy, or when we are reacting to negative energy. Reflecting negative energy creates a boundary which protects our self-love, enabling us to stay in our harmonious state. Reacting to negative energy creates attachment to the negative energy, which can only provide a disharmony.

We are redefining our energy make-up each time we react or respond to a person, or to whatever we are observing.

235

If we are to feed an ever-needed supply of self-love back into our society, we must enlighten ourselves, so we may enlighten our children. Children are our future. Children will teach their children as they have been taught. Before we can teach our children, we must learn to love and respect ourselves. When we can get *selfish* enough to take the time to love, nurture, and respect ourselves, we are well on the way to rediscovering the self-love that is naturally our birthright. When we can be kind and giving to ourselves, we can be kind and giving to our children. When we love and respect ourselves, we set that example for our children. Then we reveal what wonderful and glorious Beings we *all* truly are.

THE MAGNIFICENT ORDER OF LIFE

It is uplifting to know there truly is an order to life, a magnificent order. Life was meant to be creative, it was meant to be fun. As we come to understand that the point of connection with our Soul is love, then we can more easily turn away and starve the ego, fear-based energies. Our point of connection with our Soul is a magnificent gift that empowers our every movement. In our disconnected state, we have nothing real to offer. Each and every minute of each and every day, the most important question to ask ourselves is, "Do I feel good in this moment? Am I connected in this moment?" When we are connected, we can soak up the joy that is naturally ours and tap into our never-ending supply of God-Love-Energy. It is naturally ours, we just need to let go, relax, and let it happen. Love can envelop our every step if we simply allow it to.

We are magnificent Beings on a magnificent path, filled with creative ability. Our creative awareness begins with the magical realization of magnetism, to the fascinating truth of manifestations, to the overwhelming abundance of any dream that we can possibly imagine. We are gifted with an unlimited supply of creative energy. There is great order in the Universe. It is ours to tap into. What we can imagine, we can create. The mind is powerful, we know that, but do we know the extent of the power? Place a hundred minds in one room, each focusing on the same outcome and we will know the power. Two minds are greater than one. Three minds are greater than two, and so on. Take a moment and ponder the powerful, loving existence of the Great Energy that exists as the One Mind. If all minds come together and tap into this One Mind Power, imagine the magnetism…and imagine the outcome. It is said that when God created us in his image, a division occurred—meaning that a division of his energy took place, forming an extension of a multitude of like energies, each one being named a Soul. If this were in fact true, it would explain why the magnetism for manifestation is far greater when many minds come together focusing on the same desire.

The mind is powerful, we know that, but do we know the extent of the power?

The ego offers energy that clouds our vision. It diffuses our ability to create with ease. We are creators. But we can only create positive outcomes through a loving energy. We must tap into this loving energy if we wish to utilize our positive power of magnetism. When we take hold of our power and utilize it in the correct loving manner, we can create wonders. We can move mountains on our own. We just have to *believe*. When we come together with another individual and co-create, it is even more powerful. Imagine what thousands of people focusing on the same outcome can produce. That thought alone is fascinating.

Life is magnificent. We are creators, utilizing the energy that surrounds us, imagining it into desired form. Anything we can imagine is doable. If we can see it and *feel* it, we can have it! We each have the same gift. We are all connected to the One Universal Mind. And, as we each tap into the One Mind, we each tap into our unlimited potential!

Chapter 15

Lighting Up the Globe

YOUR UNIQUE OFFERING

Although we have all been blessed with this same God-given creative ability, it is important to realize just how this ability gives birth to each individual's uniqueness.

Each day, you are making choices in a myriad of ways that no other individual is making. Nobody else is continually thinking the exact same thoughts as you. What you think about throughout the day is creating your tomorrow. Nobody else is creating the same tomorrow as you.

This means that amongst billions of people, you alone are unique, not only in your physical make-up, but also in your creative energy make-up. Nobody in this whole world thinks like you, acts like you, or is you. All that each one of us creates makes a difference in this world. We are each blessed to be a part of this wonderful experience. We each, in our uniqueness, come together to make up a wholeness of worldly energy that contrasts and molds our global future. I call this the *Web of Life.*

Each single web within the Web of Life represents a string of energy. Each web of energy reveals the creative essence of one individual, each one forever changing and becoming, just as each individual is continually changing and becoming. All webs expand, join, and intermingle to create the overall Web of Life. Each time you make a choice, your choice impacts the overall design of the web. Our individual choices and our co-creative choices make a difference within the whole.

Everyday in the Web of Life, *you* make a difference. You create and co-create from freedom of choice. If it is your desire, you can turn away from anxiety and anger and turn toward the Light of Love. Through your freedom of choice, you are responsible for your every action and reaction.

In your unique stand, you are worthy of all that another is worthy of. You only need to *know* and *believe* in that. You are not just a number. You are a gifted existence of creative talent. You are more important than you know. It takes one individual to commence new thought. Choose your thoughts wisely and lovingly. The direction you seek can offer a difference larger than you may know.

How do you see your existence in this Web of Life? Take a moment to ponder your creative stand, and feel your unique energy make-up intermingling and influencing this fascinating Web of Life. Ponder the difference that you make each day in all the lives that surround you.

Remind yourself often, that in every step, your offering is indeed important. Your offering will add to, or deplete from, those energies that surround you. Remember, those energies that surround you are mirroring your very own energies. See through their attitudes to learn of your own reflections. If you don't like what you see, take a look at what you have been emanating.

All the released thoughts and feelings of yesterday have designed who you are today. *You are everything today as you chose to see in yourself and others yesterday.* Where you stand today, you include a complete energy make-up of the path you have created. It doesn't matter where you are today on your path, or even where you were yesterday. You are exactly where you are meant to be. Be patient and loving as you look toward tomorrow. When we can learn to live for today and enjoy this very moment in time, we can learn to love and accept who we are in our completeness.

Stand back and view this Web of Life from a distance. Note its shining beauty and soft radiant colors. As you take in this beauty, can you see the intricately molded web and how it forms and unites? Can you envision the huge span of individuals united by energy across the globe? Stand back further and visualize the countries behind the patterns. In this big beautiful world, including more than six billion individuals, feel your unique stand, and feel your unique offering. Then feel your completeness within the whole. You alone bring your own colorful essence of energy to this intricate Web of Life. Your energy does indeed make a difference!

As you emanate love and upliftment, you will be drawn to individuals who are also radiating energies of love and upliftment—highlighting together the existing colorful Light that each of you shine. Together, you will attract other seekers of the Light. The love unites, as peace presents itself and harmony is restored across the globe.

The God-Light-Energy shines brightly once again. Honor your place in this Web of Life. It is your choice in each moment to make a difference.

IT'S ALL ABOUT PEOPLE AND LOVE

When you begin to understand the Web of Life, it is easy to see the connection each Soul represents and their personal contribution in this life journey.

People are about love. It may be at a Soul level where some are not so connected to all of the time; however, love resides within each and every individual. When you choose to focus on love, you will find love. It is possible to see love in absolutely anyone. Look through to the core energy of another and see their greater meaning in your life.

See others with love and you will evoke their love!

Relationships happen at the right time, in the right place, and for the right reason. We are here to help each other learn and grow. I believe that the people we meet and the families we are born into are, for the most part, pre-determined. Also, that we have possibly intermingled with family and friends in our life today in previous lifetimes. I feel opportunities exist to meet certain people at the times we do meet, and to part at the times we do part. Also, that each individual's "growth pattern" is pre-determined via opportunities of circumstances and events that line up at the right time and in the right place.

I feel that pre-determined opportunities exist to assist us in our growth, although it is up to us how we *choose* to make use of, or react to, each of those circumstances. I call this the *Pre-Determined Dots*, just like the game *Join the Dots*. The dots are representing the pre-planned opportunity for the coming together of events and individuals. As we feel a desire come forth from within, we are being led to the next dot. Every opportunity to join each dot is provided to us via *feelings* from our Soul.

We may feel a strong desire to vacation in Italy this summer. That strong desire is our Soul sending forward an event of significance. When we follow that inner desire, we go to Rome where we end up meeting our future life partner. When we receive the desire initially, we may choose to go to Italy, or we may choose to ignore it. I feel the decision is completely in our hands. If we ignore it then further opportunity could exist to meet this person who was in Rome, as he or she might follow their Inner Guidance and end up vacationing where we live the following spring.

I feel we are always in the driver's seat, moving forward on our life's path with our Soul right there with us, navigating the way. Whether we listen to our Soul or not is ultimately our choice. But our Soul will never leave and never cease to navigate. If we follow our *feelings* within, we will not veer off our chosen path so easily.

I feel that each individual's path is designed to bring him or her toward the Light of Love and away from the fear-based ego that divides us from our God-Love-Energy. It seems as though we are led toward these *Pre-Determined Dots*. And that they will assist each of us in aligning our energy, so we may remember and reconnect to our inner truth and move toward the Light of Love.

See your family and friends as pre-chosen, Loving Beings of Light, equipped with a physical vehicle to assist them through this lifetime of growth and challenges. Then feel the way we are all intermingled and interrelated in this Web of Life. Feel and witness the loving energy within each person, then appreciate the presence of each individual in your life. For within each one, you will find mirror reflections of yourself. You will come to understand that each individual is a part of your life, and you a part of theirs, to assist each other in growing toward the Light.

LET'S MAKE A DIFFERENCE

Let's Light Up the globe with *love*. Love is worth the effort, and we each are worth the effort. We *will* all reap what we sow. When we are caring, accepting, loving, and trusting, all will be returned ten-fold. We become the essence of what we choose. My choice is to offer the Light. So, today my asking is, "Please fill me with the Light of Love and assist me in emanating it to others." I can make a difference. You can make a difference. And together, we will make a difference. As one chooses, then another, and yet another, the Light of Love will multiply across the globe.

Many people today are in pain and suffering and many are *asking* for happiness in their lives. Nothing can replace happiness, nothing at all. If we were all given one wish, we would ask to be happy right? Everything that we do, we do to make us happy. Everything that we own, we own to make us happy. Everybody that we love, we love to make us happy. When we are purely happy, we are full of love. So, in other words, happiness stems from joy, abundance, wellness, and self-worth, which equal a self-expression of love. *A self-love.* True happiness comes from loving and taking care of Self—providing Self with upliftment and fulfillment.

Whenever we are feeling happy, we are expressing love. When we express love, it is catching. Can you imagine if a lot more people would find true happiness in this world? We can make a difference if we choose. As we emanate our happiness, it will multiply and we will be rewarded with more happiness. In our happiness, we will make a difference. In years to come, the globe will surely brighten. The pace is in our hands. Can you imagine more love on this earth...then more...and then even more?

WE'RE IN THIS TOGETHER

We are all part of the One Mind. The One Mind that knows no pain, no anger, no heartache, and no bitterness. The Mind that joins and the Mind that heals. Connecting to this One Mind, where all our answers lie, means to reconnect more fully with our own Inner Guidance. As we each reconnect, we can then assist others to reconnect. We must take care of ourselves first, so we can then assist others. As we each reconnect, we join the One Mind, we become one with all, and we join the healing process.

Your partner's mind is a part of the One mind. It is important to assist your partner in reconnecting by uplifting him or her to where they wish to be. As you see others at their best, you are in that moment giving to *you* and giving to the *whole*. Each time, when you uplift yourself or another, you add to the union.

Each thought either separates us from the One Mind or joins us to the One Mind. Through focused thought, we separate or we join in each moment. All that is good is the One Mind. The One Mind continues and expands in Light Consciousness everywhere and through everything. To tap into the One Mind is seconds of focused, loving thought. To separate from the One Mind is seconds of focused anger, despair, anxiety, etc. Anything less than love separates. The One Mind exists everywhere; it exists within the ocean, the birds, and the plants. The One Mind is that of God, it is God-Love-Energy that exists absolutely everywhere. It flows through every one of us. We can tap into it, or we can tap out of it. We have free will in each moment, to join or to separate.

As we offer focused thought, we affect the whole. We are responsible for all our energy that we emanate, and we are responsible for all of our responses to all of our surroundings. Each time we respond, we cause an effect. We are all in this together. No person is more responsible than any other.

The next time someone is seeking a response from you, think before you react. Are you about to add to the whole, or are you about to separate from the whole? It is your choice in every instant, not the other person's. You have free will and can react in any way that you choose. You are indeed responsible for the energy that *you* choose to emanate. If you receive negative energy from another, and you choose in that instant to remain connected— responding from your place of love—you are in that moment setting an example for many to seek and follow. People will notice your grace and State of Well-Being, and they will silently ask to be gifted with the same.

Lighting Up the Globe

THE WAVE OF CONSCIOUSNESS—THE DOMINO EFFECT

One person emanating a loving energy can surely make a difference and add to the whole. When another sees this person feeling good and desires to feel the same, they in turn will offer their *Light,* and so it continues. Another seeker will find and ask, and another, and another. It takes just one person to set the wave in motion and cause a domino effect across the globe. True happiness is catching. If you can offer but one person your *Light of Love,* you have affected the whole. Our minds are all "one" on the higher realm. When we choose and hold on to a lesser energy, we separate from the whole. When we choose our truth and hold to it, we join energies with the whole. Our moment-to-moment choice either offers a separation or offers a union.

The wave of consciousness will continue to manifest, even if we choose in the next moment to separate ourselves from the whole. The people we have previously affected remain affected and have moved on to offer their *Light* to other seekers. We may know in the moment that we are affecting another when we hold an understanding of Light versus dark. However, even in our unaware state, we can still affect and uplift another when we are communicating through our connected state, with our inner truth.

We can add to the *Light* and make a difference. When we consciously add to the Light, we then become the *Light Workers.* As Light Workers, we consciously make a difference. We do not need words to make a difference. We only need to be in our connected, loving state. As we, the Light Workers, emanate our Light in our aware state, we are deliberately creating a rippling effect within the wave of consciousness. We are assisting to bring Light and growth to the whole.

To become a Light Worker within this wave of consciousness is a choice from our heart. When this is our choice, then it is a matter of making a conscious effort to turn away from flaws. Also, to allow others to miscreate in their unawareness if that is their *choice,* or to offer our knowledge when we feel the *asking.* And to allow ourselves to make mistakes along the way, taking responsibility for all of our magnetized attractions. Above all, to stand by in our peaceful state, knowing our emanation of peace is offered as fruits from the sweetest tree. Reminding ourselves daily to accept and allow, accept and allow. Of course, for our own self-esteem, it is important to always maintain self-respect and boundaries; and in turn, we will naturally emanate those qualities to others.

When another is miscreating, yet not seeking to do otherwise, we can reflect and allow while turning the other cheek. We only need to implement our boundaries when a negative energy is directed at us. As we accept and allow another to be all they need to be, offering upliftment either through positive words or a peaceful, happy stand, we are revealing our personal power through our unconditional offering of love. We are in that moment a Light Worker making a difference to the whole.

In our acceptance and allowance, we offer our faith and our truth. We know that "all is truly well."

MASS CONSCIOUSNESS

One mind of one individual makes a difference larger than we may know. When two minds of two individuals come together to form a similar goal, the power of attraction is greater than if it were just one mind of one individual. When a large gathering of individuals comes together all desiring a similar goal—the magnetic attraction is powerfully amplified.

A mass conscious energy shift involves a group of dedicated individuals and can occur at any time and in any place. These dedicated individuals are Light Workers, and these Light Workers hold enough passion and faith to assist in shifting energy. The more individuals involved, the greater the mind power that exists. The more mind power, the more positive energy produced, meaning an alignment for manifestation is formed at a more rapid rate. The more passion put forth to shift energy and bring about the change, the greater the aligning power. More individuals with the same desire supplies more passion. Passionate energy is creative energy.

The attraction power of multiple minds is expansive.

If your desire is to bring together a group of Light Workers, then simply *ask* for the Light Workers to come forward. Visit your local church, or talk to family members and friends. The right individuals will come forward to assist at the right time. When your gathering comes together, choose an individual to lead the group— an individual who is quite dedicated to the outcome.

The chosen individual would lead the group by first stating the desire at hand. The desire, for example, might be for the healing of a sick individual (in which case it is most effective for the sick person to be present and involved in the prayer), or to save an endangered species, or to save local parkland that the city wants to turn into a multi-level parking lot. The leader, after stating the overall desire, would then ask the group to give thoughts and intention toward the desired result. He or she would then lead the group through prayer, offering encouraging words, while always focusing on a positive result.

We *can* come together to assist in magnetizing positive energy toward a desired result. It doesn't matter what the desire is, as long as the group has *passion* and *faith* toward the desired result. Passion and faith can move mountains; they are what exist at the basis of all miracles.

When we ask for the healing of another individual, we are in that moment seeing them in the *Light* we know they wish to be seen. As we have discussed, we do not create for any other; however, we can *influence* another individual when we see them in good health. It is most important though, that the seeker of healing have a *strong desire* to be healed. This is usually the case when a group has come together to pray for healing, as the initial *desire* for healing by the seeker *attracted* the Light Workers in the first place. At the basis of healing is the seeker's own initial desire coupled with their faith that causes the shift to occur. Additionally, Light Workers, through their power of loving energy, send forth their passion and faith; which in turn, evokes the seeker's passion and faith, which maximizes the power placed toward the healing process. The more passion and faith sent forth from the Light Workers, the more passion and faith can be evoked from the seeker of healing, thus creating a greater energy shift.

HEALING THE WORLD

We can each assist in healing the world. When the ego is shed, as a snake sheds its old skin, the fullness of Soul will surface. Love can heal the world and love will heal the world. Love brings heaven to earth and unites us with the glory of all goodness. We each have the ability to make a difference. We each have the ability to offer a healing power. When we release the old conditional mindset and relax into our unconditional knowing that all is truly well—all will be truly well. We only need to open our hearts and allow the healing to occur. When we believe that love heals, then we will know to turn the other cheek from everything else that is less than love.

The wave has been set in motion, the domino effect has begun, and the world is healing. The turn of the millennium brought about a major energy shift. In the past ten years, spiritual growth has rapidly increased in large numbers. The self-help and spiritual sections in bookstores have proven this to be so. The shift is occurring as Light Workers are spreading their *Light* across the globe.

As more and more get *selfish* enough to take care of their own love first, their own love will overspill and Light Up the Way for others. We need to heal ourselves first by shedding the old skin and remembering our truth. Through our reconnection, we *will* remember our truth. We will remember why we are here, and we will create and co-create like the true creators that we are. Through our self-adoration and belief, we will shine our *Light* and set an example of pure love. We will make a difference larger than we can even know. Together, we *can* bring heaven to earth and heal the world.

THE TEACHER WITHIN

As we grow toward the Light, we have so much to offer others. We can make a difference by offering our knowledge of love to the world and then visualizing seekers entering our door.

When people ask you what you have learned then you become the *teacher*. They have been brought to you, for you have offered the world your knowledge of love. If you feel in your heart a desire to offer your love on a larger scale, then you can definitely make a larger difference. Continue to *ask* for your students and appreciate their willingness to learn.

If you begin to feel drained as you are helping others then take time out and give yourself a break. Remember to keep your self-love fulfilled. Always take care of Self first. When you are fulfilled, your self-love will overflow and you will have much love to offer this world.

We are each on our own path and will seek in our own way. We can accept others as they are and respect their choices by answering only when they are seeking. Remember to wait for the "asking." When someone is appearing lost and you feel you know the answer, it is useless information unless the confused person is *asking*. You will know when someone is asking, it may be directly or indirectly, but nonetheless you will feel it in his or her energy; and you will know in your heart if it feels right to deliver the information. When you deliver the answer and it is received with love, you will *feel* it in your heart. You are in that moment the Light Worker, *Lighting the Path to Love* and adding *Light* to the Web of Life.

It doesn't matter what you choose to do. If you prefer to remain the silent type and emanate your self-love naturally, then you are already making a larger difference than you know. Others will read your harmonious state, and as they *enjoy* being in your presence, they will silently ask for the same.

We are all teachers and we are all students. When we hear an asking, we become the teacher. When we are doing the asking, we become the student. At no point, for the remainder of our lifetime, will we become only one, either the student or the teacher. There will always be a shift from one to the other. We must learn as we move in time so we can *know,* and what we *know* we will teach; whether it be through words or through our energy that we emanate. We can offer respect for student and teachers alike. Everyone deserves respect no matter where they are at in their lives. Whether they are in a hole and can't get out, or have hit a wall and can't walk through. Or whether they are walking on water, or have grown wings and can fly. We are all in this together and we all need understanding and upliftment along the way, especially when we are not in a position to give it to ourselves.

We each assist one another in moving toward the Light.

You are gifted as I have been gifted with the knowledge set forth in this book. Taking forth this knowledge, you become the teacher. Believe in yourself as you Light Up the Way. Believe in yourself as you share your learning. You are amazing in your own Light, whether it be a good day or a bad day, or whether you are giving the Light or receiving the Light. Allow yourself to just *be,* and know that you are so worthy. As the student, you are worthy, for you are receiving the messages so you may turn into the teacher. As the teacher, you are worthy, for you are preparing the students to teach.

Thus the Light awakens in another, and then in another, and continues like a domino effect throughout mankind in our silent path of our Spiritual Awakening.

Chapter 16

The Greatest Gift

AWAKENING TO THE BEAUTY WITHIN

Taking time to smell the roses is not unlike taking the time to feel your true beauty resonate from within. We must *choose* to take the time to stop and taste the sweetness of true beauty. Take a deep breath and as you inhale, taste the sweetness in awakening to the truth that your Soul surely does exist within. As you exhale, relax into the knowing that your Soul will always be there.

We have the ability to tap into God-Love-Energy whenever we choose. Our Soul doesn't rest. It does not need rest, for it resides in pure, loving energy. What makes us tired is disconnection, which is brought about from fear-based energy. The Soul works and delivers information while we slumber. It is forever one hundred percent bound to our human form. It will not leave the body until death occurs, for that is when the Soul is no longer required to feed knowledge and support through the body. But remember, the Soul is truly who *we* are. The body is our vehicle. When we are resting behind the wheel of the car in a dazed driving position, it is said that our Soul takes over and drives the car. When we are *that* relaxed and connected, our Soul can shine through and take over. We *are* that which shines through. The number of life after death experiences that have been recorded around the world give a strong indication that we really do see through the eyes of our Soul. In many of these cases recorded, individuals have stated that during their death experience they rose above their body and looked back down at their body. This can only be if they are seeing through the eyes of a source other than their human eyes. And, because many have stated that they felt it was truly their own Self as they exited their body, is indication they were quite possibly seeing through the eyes of their Soul.

When we can grasp the truth that we do indeed have a Soul that guides us, and fathom the possibility that we truly are this Soul living through a perfectly created human form, is when a whole new world of opportunity opens. This is the way it was supposed to be. Our Soul chose its human form and its parents. Our Soul is our beauty that exists within. When we relax, let go, and have faith, our Soul can completely shine through.

Awakening to our beauty within is recognizing that we truly do have this amazing, positive, loving energy inside of us. It is in understanding that we are able to connect to it at any time. It is in the knowing that this is our only truth, and that there is no outer truth that knows something our Soul does not know.

RECOGNIZING THE GIFT

Your connected state with your Soul sends a flow of good feeling energy through your body and helps you to feel wonderful. Your good feeling energy is precious. It is a gift. As you go about your day, take notice of the way you are feeling. Know in each moment that the way you *feel* affects you and also your surroundings. It is important to bring good energy to the table, as our own energy is the only true contribution that we really have to offer anybody or anything in this life. I say *anybody,* as our energy is able to affect all those we come into contact with. I say *anything,* as our energy is able to affect material items we have manifested into our life as well.

For example:

Alex was driving home from work after a bad day at the office, when his car stopped twice in the middle of the street. It started again; however, at that point, Alex was already having a bad day and complained to himself about his car breaking down the whole way home. Alex then complained to his wife when he arrived home. He complained again later that evening when he spoke with a friend on the phone. The next morning, Alex's car that he offered all of that negative energy toward broke down halfway to the office, and this time it needed towing. Alex was, at the time, heading to an extremely important, one-time meeting that could not be rescheduled.

Granted, the car had a problem and required fixing, but if the negative energy offered weren't quite so powerful, the car breaking down most likely would have taken place at a far better time. Also, if Alex had let go of the bothersome thoughts—meaning he would have remained connected—he may then have been *led* to arrange an appointment to have his car looked over and taken alternate transportation that morning instead.

Our energy affects the whole and everything within the whole, including our loved ones, our own selves, and all that is manifested within our existence. We add to, or we take away from, the *whole* in every ounce of energy that we offer. Our energy affects everything—absolutely everything!

Our energy is a gift and we must nurture our energy for us to maintain a healthy life in all areas. Recognizing our energy as a gift and its importance to all of our surroundings is recognizing our responsibility in emanating our Light.

NURTURING YOUR LOVE FOR SELF

It is important to recognize your energy as a gift *within* and to nurture it. Your energy affects you and your surroundings in every way. The way you feel throughout the day adds to who you are, or depletes who you are. If you allow yourself to become depleted by giving of yourself until you have nothing left to give, then you are in essence zapping your own energy. No other can create for you and no other can truly take away from you. It is in your own choice that you offer your energy for the taking. YOU decide how to utilize and distribute *your* energy in each step. Energy is precious. It is so worth the effort to nurture and take care of *your* energy.

Let's take a look at an example of Jill nurturing her energy:

Jill was on her way to an event in San Diego, where she was to be one of the main speakers. Jill had a long drive, as she lived in Los Angeles. On her way, she felt very relaxed. She had given herself ample time to make it to the event on time, so she could arrive relaxed and be well prepared to deliver an uplifting presentation. She played some of her favorite music and daydreamed about the weekend coming up.

When Jill arrived at the event, she was feeling wonderful; however, when she entered the ballroom, she immediately felt a low energy within the room. She soon found out that right before she arrived, the head organizer and the caterer of the event had gotten into a disagreement. They were obviously still upset with each other. Jill decided she was in a wonderful mood and she would stay that way, not allowing anything to upset her that morning. She was feeling so good and didn't want to lose this wonderful feeling. The organizer walked over to where Jill stood and attempted to tell Jill what had happened ten minutes prior. Jill at once decided to protect her precious, good feeling energy and remove herself from the conversation. Jill politely explained to the organizer that she had some papers to look over and would need to excuse herself until the commencement of the event. Jill exited the ballroom and found a quiet place to sit and read over her papers while waiting for the event to commence.

When Jill returned to the ballroom, she was feeling wonderful, relaxed, and ready to offer a well-prepared, energetic presentation. She felt grateful that she had taken care of her precious energy and now had an uplifting energy to offer the students seated in front of her.

Our good feeling energy is a precious gift. When we are feeling good energy within, we are connected to God-Love-Energy. Why would we ever want to be disconnected when being connected feels *so* wonderful?

Not only does connection feel wonderful, it also frees up our energy so the door remains open and all manifestations continue to flow through.

Nobody can nurture our energy except for ourselves. Others may influence our energy and offer us insight regarding our magnificence, however, the ultimate choice is always our own. Another can *offer* us nurturing words. Another can *offer* us the golden keys. Whether or not we decide to embrace those words and turn the keys to unlock our greatest truth and potential is completely up to ourselves.

We are responsible for the way that we feel in each moment. In keeping our energy feeling wonderful, it is important to reflect surrounding negative energy whenever and wherever we can. When a negative energy is directed straight at us, it is sometimes difficult to ignore it. However, all energy that we are witnessing is always mirroring our own energy, whether or not we are currently feeling negative, or whether we were feeling that way yesterday. We must understand that we clearly invited this energy from our previous thoughts. When we take responsibility and cease to blame others for what we are witnessing, is when we will begin to notice negative energy less and less as time goes by. What we don't offer focus to must cease to exist, for we are no longer feeding that same negative energy.

Soon enough, we will come to realize just how precious our good feeling energy is and begin to nurture it. All we need to do is *ask* for assistance in taking care of our precious energy and our connectedness, and we will be *led* to do so.

The Greatest Gift

GIVING THANKS

It is important to be thankful for everything that has come into our life that gives us joy. When we feel appreciation, we are feeding our creation and will be blessed with further enjoyment of that very creation. When we tend to take things for granted, they either leave our life or just stay stagnant and block room for growth.

It is natural to love and appreciate something that brings us joy. However, as time goes by, many of us tend to take items or persons for granted. We forget to stop and *feel* appreciative for their existence in our lives. If we wish for something we have created to stay, grow, and thrive in our lives, we must feed it with appreciation and love.

Appreciation is energy of love. Feed your creations with your energy of love. Love is like a flower. It is delicate, yet strong in its ability to thrive under many conditions. The more love you give, the more alive and vibrant your creations will become. So feed all the things you appreciate in your life with love of appreciation, and watch them grow and continue to give you joy.

Take a few moments now and feel the appreciation for the joyful aspects in your life. Feel their value. Enjoy their presence. Feel the upliftment in your appreciation. Take a piece of paper and write down five items or persons that you give thanks for today. Beside each one, state why you would like that particular item or person to stay in your life.

Next, on a separate piece of paper, list all the qualities you appreciate in yourself. For example, you might feel appreciative for your honesty, your independency, your happiness, your wisdom, or your humor.

It is important to stop and take a look at the wonderful things in life and feel merciful for their existence. To be thankful creates growth. Each day, for just one minute, recall one of the wondrous blessings you have received and feel appreciation for this item or person. You will be surprised how a little appreciation can make a big difference. Just one item, for one minute, each day.

Giving thanks and feeling appreciation *prior* to receiving any desired manifestation creates a loving, clear path for receiving our manifestation. When we give thanks with the feeling of appreciation prior to receiving a manifestation, it sets forth a passionate energy of having already *received* the manifestation. Each day, offer thanks and feel appreciative for those desires or goals that you hold, and watch them flow into your life.

YOUR GREATEST GIFT—YOUR SELF-LOVE

Owning *self-love* is the answer to living a life full of passion, harmony, connection, upliftment, and magical grace. *Self-love* provides for the *happiness* that we all do crave.

If you were to ask yourself, "What is my greatest wish in my life today?"—what do you think it would be? Ponder the question for a minute and see what rises from within. No matter what words you come up with, I am sure you can derive the word happiness from them. At the basis of all prayer is the desire for happiness.

True happiness *begins* within. Go to the place where all of your answers lie. Learn to trust in your feelings. They hold the golden answers to life. When you follow your feelings, you will find true happiness. When you follow your feelings, you will find freedom. When you follow your feelings, you will remain connected to your Soul and to the magical power of the Universe.

Never underestimate the power of your Soul—the power is within you! Your Soul knows all of your desires, therefore knows where to take you and what to show you. Your Soul knows what will make you happy. Your Soul knows what clothes you wish to wear. Your Soul knows what weight you would like to be. Your Soul knows what to eat, what not to eat, and how much to eat so you can be the size you love to be. Your Soul knows what you liked yesterday and what you don't like today.

Your Soul knows the total energy make-up of that which you emanate. Your Soul knows every thought that you think. It knows where you have been, not just in this lifetime, but also in many other lifetimes. It knows where you are heading on your life path. Your Soul is intuitive energy, therefore it knows your future before it manifests. When you are listening, your Soul will whisper how events will unfold before they unfold. It will give you signals how to handle events and people before the day arrives, and again moments before. Your Soul whispers to you, every minute, of every day. When you get quiet and listen, you will *know*. Your Soul sends feelings each time you wonder, ponder, or ask. Your Soul always replies with a feeling. Whether you are paying attention or not, your Soul still replies. Your Soul doesn't stop communicating with you; however, through freedom of choice, you can cease to communicate with your Soul.

When you harmonize with yourself, you are harmonizing with your Soul. You can live through your truth when you live through your Soul. When you connect with your

Soul, you connect with everything. Our Soul forms our union and moves us beyond separation to the totality of All-That-Is. To connect with our Soul connects us to God. When our Soul shines through us, God is shining through us.

Your greatest gift shines from within. There is nothing more valuable in the entire Universe. Nothing will bring greater happiness than your love that surges through your body. There is nothing more divine. Stand tall. Stand proud. Stand firm. Connect to your truth and be the powerful creator that you truly are. This book offers an opportunity to unlock the door to your desires, to move forward with a new thought process, and walk a path toward enlightenment and divinity.

Scoop up your treasures of life, for it is okay to receive. It is okay to dream all you can dream. It is okay to have all you can hold. It is okay to give it all away. Energy is forming and molding and turning into matter all the time. Energy extends and forms continually. There is plenty of energy to go around. There are plenty of manifestations to be formed. Riches are everywhere. There is enough for everyone and then some. Riches don't pop out of nowhere. They are manifested through sequences of thought and revolving energy. If each of us utilize these golden keys and create riches, each of us will be wealthy. The opportunity to manifest is within our every thought. Our continued focus of passionate thought molds and forms the energy to give birth to the manifestation. It makes no difference whether it is material or non-material, or if the steps to get there involve two people or two hundred people. Energy aligns and brings like-minded co-creators together to experience the outcome of their choosing.

We each hold the same creative ability to imagine and develop whatever we wish to hold. Every living thing, every conversation, and every object commenced from one thought! Everything in our existence, material or non-material, initiated from thought! As we appreciate and offer loving thoughts to the people and items around us, they stay and they grow. As we cease to appreciate and cease to offer loving thoughts, people and items may leave our surroundings. *Loving thoughts* are what create ongoing positive, uplifting, *loving* surroundings.

Here are the golden keys, and if it is your wish then here is the door, and just up ahead, there is the gateway to the life you came here to create. Enjoy your riches. Enjoy your nothings, for riches and nothing are one. We are only ever one step away from where we are wishing to be. Attitude is everything. Right now, in our joy or in our sorrow, we are right where we are meant to be. Tomorrow, whether we choose joy or sorrow, we are again right where we are meant to be. Energy is forever transforming and becoming. We get to where we want to be from falling at times. Sometimes we must know the negative to ask for the positive.

Don't beat yourself up if you are feeling down today. It is okay. Bless your current stand, for as you now stand, you can create from a new place of awareness. Learn to be okay with where you stand today. For where you stand today is your truth. No matter what, you are never on your own. When we connect to God-Love-Energy then we connect to everything. When we disconnect, our Soul is still right there with us feeding the information and working at getting our attention and reconnection.

Connection, whether it is to an object or to Spirit is the same thing. When we connect to our Soul and All-That-Is, we connect to everything because it is all united through the loving energy of God. The energy that surrounds us and lives through all the plants, animals, soils, sun, and rain is the energy of God. When we are connected, riches and nothing become the same. The imagination can take many directions. The attitude can also take many directions. Freedom of choice is ours in every moment. If we can even slightly grasp the imagination and positive attitude that is our right, then we can soar to possibilities not fathomed by many in society today.

Earth is a playground. It is *our* playground. We created it, all of us, because we are all part of the same. We created our total existence, and we are re-creating it in every minute of every day. We can join and create with love, or we can separate and create with fear. Those who join with the whole and create for the most part with love will live happily every after. Those who separate from the whole and create for the most part with fear will undoubtedly live in pain.

The glory of giving is right at your fingertips. It is not monetary or material. It is your very own pure, loving energy that you have to offer. Yes, the best things in life are free! When you are feeling great about Self and emanating your self-love, you are in that moment giving the greatest gift you have to offer...*your self-love.*

The Greatest Gift

The greatest gift that you can give yourself today is your self-love!

The greatest gift that you can give to any other is your self-love!

Now you hold the golden keys to open the gateway and *connect* more fully with your Soul; to implement your faith, boundaries, self-respect, self-worth, and creative ability.

As you implement these attributes and walk joyously forward on your new path, you will move into a higher realm, where you will develop and harmonize with your greatest gift...*your self-love.*

As you feel your self-love, your greatest gift within, go forth with emanation. Reveal your *Light of Love* to the world. The world is waiting. You are the teacher. *And always remember...be selfish enough to nurture your own self-love!*

Joy To The Journey

Joy to the journey, the Soul has come;
Ignite to the world, rejoice everyone.
The path may be distant and seem at times dark...
But the fruit comes alive when our Souls come to spark.
Deliver the love and watch it go around,
Open the Universe and magic we've found.
A message to all..."let the journey begin"...
Light up the globe and light the passion within.
Souls know the journey so allow them to soar,
And feel our own laughter forever more.